AF505998

SUNSET OF THE EMPIRE IN MALAYA

SUNSET OF THE EMPIRE IN MALAYA

A New Zealander's Life in the Colonial Education Service

T.K. Taylor

The Radcliffe Press

LONDON • NEW YORK

Published in 2006 by The Radcliffe Press
6 Salem Road, London W2 4BU

In the United States and in Canada
distributed by Palgrave Macmillan, a division of St Martin's Press
175 Fifth Avenue, New York NY 10010

ISBN 1 84511 111 7
EAN 978 1 84511 111 3

A full CIP record for this book is available from the British Library
A full CIP record for this book is available from the Library of Congress

Library of Congress Catalog card: available

Typeset in India by Digital Publishing Solutions
Printed and bound in Great Britain by MPG Books Ltd, Bodmin

In grateful memory of Yvonne's partnership throughout
the years of this account

Contents

Acknowledgements

It is essential to give some explanation of the author's indebtedness to his daughter, Alice, and to Associate Professor Penny McKay, our friend of many years, because without their support and very great assistance the work would never have been completed.

Alice has looked after our home since her mother died in 1991 and hence I have been able to live in my home of many years, which of course contains all the records and books relating to my life and career. Alice trains library technicians at the Sydney Institute of Technology, and produced a typed version of the first draft of this book.

As author, I have pleasure in expressing my deep appreciation of all Penny's assistance in preparing the work for publication. Circumstances have delayed further attention since I wrote the first draft in 1992, so Penny's advice and expertise have been invaluable in the necessary adaptations for publication. In all fields of endeavour, attitudes change continually, and it seems to the me that present opinions about the British Empire are more objective than they were in the recent past. Penny's familiarity with current publishing techniques is of great value, and I am most fortunate in having her experience in this regard. But as usual in any work, I wish to emphasise that the responsibility for the statements and opinions is entirely mine.

T.K. Taylor
January 2002

Foreword

When Tom Taylor asked me to help complete this book, I was more than willing to do so. I stepped in only after he and his daughter, Alice, had done most of the work. Having heard some of Tom's stories about Malaya, I have recognised for a long time that they are stories that should be recorded formally and made available to family members and historians.

I have particular pleasure in providing a foreword to the book because my own parents, George and Peggy Harvey, were in Malaya at the same time as the Taylors. My father was serving as a British Army officer in Jahore Bahru. We three Harvey children were the same age as the Taylor children, and our two families have maintained a strong friendship since that time. I can therefore say that I have known Tom for almost 50 years, and feel well able to introduce him, and this book.

The first thing that strikes one about Tom is his remarkable memory. He has an ability to recall immediately dates, names and figures, not only from his own experiences, but from history and current events. A question to Tom about an event in history is likely to evoke (if Tom is encouraged) a lengthy, interesting and accurate lecture on the subject. This book therefore comes directly out of Tom's memories of Malaya, supplemented by photographs that he has also been able to describe by place, names and specific date.

Tom's second characteristic was shared by his dear wife, Yvonne, who died in Sydney in December 1991. Tom and Yvonne have built their lives around family and close friendships. They had four children of their own, but 'adopted' a number of additional sons and daughters. I was honoured to be Daughter Number 5, and was welcomed into the home as such many times over the years – and still am today. Tom still receives around 60 Christmas cards every year, from every corner of the world, reflecting the number of people they have met and kept as friends over the years.

The third characteristic I would like to point out is dedication. I mention this characteristic from my own observations of their work in the 1960s in Perth, Western Australia, when Tom was involved in library administration and Yvonne was teaching (and I was welcomed into the family on a working holiday). Both Tom and Yvonne

were totally dedicated to their work, to the people they worked for
and to the people they worked with. Both were skilled teacher train-
ers. Yvonne was an outstanding organiser and Tom an excellent
administrator. Their dedication to their work and the people they
were responsible for shines through this account and through the
many photographs they have of their time in Malaya and is evident
in their rise to high ranks in the British Colonial Service.

This foreword, then, is a personal introduction from one who has
been honoured to have known Tom and his family. It is very apt that
Tom and Yvonne's time in Malaya, at a critical period when modern
Malaya was emerging after the Second World War, is recorded for
future generations.

Associate Professor Penny McKay
January 2002
Brisbane, Australia

Preface

The prime purpose of this account is to provide, for my children and their descendants, a personal statement of my life, of my attitude to my work and to the events of daily life therein, as they occurred. It is therefore limited in essence to events which I actually witnessed, or to wider developments in which I shared some part of the responsibility and action, and to my own views on these occurrences. All else, as far as possible, I have tried to limit to what is needed to understand the above narrative. My perspectives are those of a person living and working in the British colonies in the 1940s and 1950s.

No claim is made for any personal special ability or achievement, or for any unusual feature in any individual event or circumstance. As will be evident, I have found my lifetime experience interesting and, all in all, count myself fortunate in the general course of occurrences as they unfolded. For years my wife and family have expressed a keen desire that a memoir should be written, but circumstances have not been accommodating. A further consideration has been the desire expressed by the Oxford Colonial Archives Project, Rhodes House Library, Oxford, for records of the careers of officers who served in the Colonial Empire in the various Territories before they received independence.

The information on the history of the British Empire, of which the States of Malaya formed a part, is given as a background to the years when my wife, Yvonne, and I lived and worked in the country. By rendering this account, I have of course tried to state my own attitude to the events described, thereby hoping to bring those events into clearer focus. I have noted in the 'Bibliographical note'[1] a reference to the item in question where this seemed desirable or helpful.

An endeavour will be made to make the narrative cogent and self-explanatory, and to make plain the connection of the events with the general theme. However, it may be mentioned that the question most commonly asked of me has been, 'How did it happen that you came to serve in Malaya?' I did not know anyone in New Zealand who joined the Colonial Service, and furthermore, most of the recruits from New Zealand to the Service went to one of the African colonies, which in effect made up the bulk of the Territories controlled by the Colonial Office. It can only be supposed that a tradition had developed along these lines, and of course vacancies in posts under the African Governments would form the majority of colonial positions on offer at any one time.

Thus it was that the choice of Malaya was that of myself and my wife after we studied the brochure 'RDW6' circulated by the Colonial Office to the various wartime services. Malaya was closer to New Zealand than Africa, and I had associated in the RNZAF with Malayan officers who spoke most highly, and fondly, of the country. I have always been grateful to them.

The 'Bibliographical note' includes not only those sources which refer to statements made in the course of the narrative, but also to various works to which I have referred for information connected with my work, and to others which came to my notice while writing this narrative. My assumption is that at any time in the future there will be available in libraries reliable works on the history of the Empire and of the times of which I write, to supply the enquiring reader with the additional information needed. At the same time, I have attempted to give sufficient historical background to enable the reader to understand how and why the events described occurred as they did, without having recourse to any work of reference. How far I have succeeded, each reader must decide for him or herself.

Tom Taylor
Sydney, Australia
June 2001

Prologue: the British Empire

This memoir would not have been written if the Empire had never existed. It is now over 30 years since the final remnant of the official organisation was abolished when the Colonial Office was closed in 1966. But many of the conditions and much of the political character of the countries of the present day stem directly from the influence and development of the Empire during its existence. Not irrelevant either is the occurrence in 1992 of the semi-millennium of the discovery of America by Christopher Columbus.

The age of discovery was pioneered by the Portuguese, who were followed by the other maritime countries of Western Europe, Spain, Holland, France and England, who each founded trading settlements or made conquests in the regions that each country had explored. The voyages of Columbus (1492) for Spain, and Vasco da Gama (1497) for Portugal, were followed by vast activities by these sea-faring powers in the next century.

Actually, a Venetian explorer, John Cabot, sailed from Bristol in 1497 and reached the continent of North America under a patent from King Henry VII a year before Columbus arrived at the mainland. The voyages by John Cabot and his son Sebastian later resulted in the annexation of Newfoundland, England's first colony, which was important for the fishing industry. During the sixteenth century the English founded several trading companies, such as those to the Levant and to Russia, the most important, the East India Company, being founded in 1600.

Colonies have been established by different states down the centuries usually for one or more of three purposes: as trading posts; in strategic positions to guard trade routes; and as settlements for surplus population. Contrary to common belief, including that of the Greeks themselves, the ancient Greeks, mainly in the eighth to sixth centuries BC, established many colonies right around the Mediterranean and Black Seas for all of these purposes, singly or in combination, and not only as settlements.

As in so much else in European civilisation, the Greeks initiated a trend and carried out to a highly successful conclusion the establishment of well over a thousand settlements, most of them quite tiny, but including some major military powers such as Syracuse in

Sicily. Quite often, as is widely known, the small states in mainland Greece and its archipelago often ran out of space and resources to support the existing populations and new communities were established where a site could be found. Of course, the process often brought the invaders into contention with the existing inhabitants, sometimes settled by negotiation, sometimes by armed conflict. The Greeks were at the time the most advanced in the arts of civilisation, so their advent often brought benefits to the local populations, not least in wealth from trade, and this fact often made them acceptable to the other peoples. The colonial activities of the British lasted from about 1600 to the middle of the twentieth century, and many parallels can be drawn with the Greek experience.

The Portuguese, French and Dutch acquired or founded localities as trading posts, which of course had to have defences. From these developed French Quebec and the Dutch settlements in the Cape Colony and the East Indies, in none of which settled a large population from the colonial power. The Spanish acquired a vast empire in America, and the Portuguese the control of Brazil as well as trading posts in the East, the exploitation of which was the main economic concern of the two powers in succeeding centuries.

The migration[2] of large populations overseas in modern times is therefore a mainly British phenomenon, whereas in ancient times it was that of the Greeks. The first American colony, Virginia, was founded in 1607, followed by colonies established by religious sects – New England, Puritans; Maryland, Catholics; Pennsylvania, Quakers. The southern colonies were founded as plantations growing tobacco, sugar and cotton; while New York, established by the Dutch as a trading post, was a prize of war in 1664. A point often overlooked is that several American colonies were established as a protest against policies of the English Government. The Puritans in particular attempted to make their colony of Massachusetts independent quite soon after establishment by transferring its charter, granted by James I, from London to Boston. This colony was in fact operating independently during the Civil War in the 1640s, until Oliver Cromwell sent over a fleet to demand compliance with imperial rules. Of course the colonies were for a long time dependent on England for protection, for trade and for supplies generally.

The famous 'Boston Tea Party' at the time of American independence was not a sudden emanation of independent ambitions. The important factor in ensuring the progress of the colonies was the ready availability of ample good food, which was not available to the common people in the mother country when the colonies were established and for many years thereafter. After the early grim years – the thousand inhabitants of Virginia in 1625 were the survivors of five times that number of migrants, and most of the 'Pilgrim Fathers' died the year after they arrived in 1620 – soon the American colonies were doubling their population in each generation.

Perhaps the most remarkable colonial enterprise of all was the settlement of Sydney. Despite the early hardship in New South Wales, when Macquarie left in 1822 the condition of the colonists in every material aspect was much in advance of that of the contemporary industrial cities in England.[3] Thus it was quite common early in the 1820s, and even before, for people to commit a crime in England in order to be transported to Botany Bay, that is, New South Wales.

Of concern to me, New Zealand was established as a British colony in 1840 by the Treaty of Waitangi, which was signed by all the chiefs of the Maori tribes. At the present time of course this treaty is being used by the Maoris to gain concessions, which is a common situation wherever there are large indigenous populations as in North America or Australia. Similar to the eastern Australian colonies, New Zealand made rapid progress, initially from the wool industry, then from other farm products – meat, butter, cheese – with a great boost in the 1860s from large gold discoveries. New Zealand received self-government in 1855, along with New South Wales, South Australia, Tasmania and Victoria.

The gold discoveries were at first made in the South Island, which caused this island to advance rapidly; roads and railways were extended, and Dunedin and Christchurch developed into cities of some substance, economically as well as culturally. For example, the University of Otago, the first in New Zealand, was established in 1868, and Canterbury University College in Christchurch in 1873.

Differences over land rights with the Maoris in the North Island, where nearly all Maoris live, erupted into active warfare in the 1860s. When peace came, the government endeavoured to give the North Island the facilities already in place in the South Island, which was helped by gold discoveries in the Auckland Province. A scheme of Assisted Immigration was introduced in the 1870s, which considerably augmented the population.[4]

From about 1885 to 1895 there was a severe economic depression and it was not until 1900 that the population in the North Island overtook that of the South Island. Today three quarters of the population of over three million live in the North Island. The development of refrigeration in the 1890s enabled a large export trade in meat, butter and cheese to be developed. Assisted Immigration was resumed after 1900 and by the outbreak of the First World War, New Zealand (measured by GNP) was one of the most prosperous countries in the 'western world', exceeded only by Australia.

Events in Malaya will also be the subject of extensive coverage in this memoir. The first British contact with Malaya was in 1786, when the East India Company purchased the island of Penang from the Sultan of Kedah, together with a strip of the mainland opposite, named Province Wellesley. A young clerk, Thomas Stamford Raffles, was appointed to the Penang office in 1805 and became Chief Secretary in 1807.

Malacca was taken over from the Dutch in 1795, when Holland had been overrun during the French advance into Europe in the war with revolutionary France which began in 1793. Singapore Island was obtained by Raffles from the Sultan of Johore in 1819. Malacca was finally ceded to Britain by treaty from the Dutch in 1824. These three small possessions became the Straits Settlements, a British colony under a governor in Singapore, and eventually the foundation of British influence in the Malay Peninsula, which was divided into a number of small Malay States.

Malaya is extremely mountainous, only small areas of arable land being available along coastal strips or in river valleys. Before European arrival, the rivers provided the only means of communication and transport, and the limited resources supported only a small population, mainly Malays with a small minority of primitive aboriginal tribes, totalling a few tens of thousands of people in each State, ruled by a traditional autocratic sultan.

Before 1880, the main developments had been, first, the capture of Malacca by the Portuguese in 1511, who in turn were overcome by the Dutch in 1631, who in turn were superseded by the British in 1795. The town of Malacca, and a surrounding area of about 20 miles in each direction, was therefore under European rule for almost four and a half centuries, and with the other Portuguese bases, Goa in India and Macao in China, is among the oldest European settlements in Asia.

The other important development was the tin industry, which was worked by the Chinese before the capture of Malacca. The industry, mainly situated along the rivers of Perak and Selangor, gave the rulers of these States a source of revenue superior to those of the other States. However, the proneness of the Chinese to develop separate antagonistic factions, derived from origins in China or from secret societies, caused considerable difficulty, the Malays not having police forces to ensure order. Tradition has it that perennial strife in an important tin mining area, Taiping in North Perak, was finally resolved by the parties agreeing on a permanent peaceful arrangement, cementing it by bestowing the name Taiping on the locality – a Chinese term for 'peace'. The Malays have accepted this name for the town to this day.

British influence, developing into an effective administrative control over the Federated and other Malay States, was remarkably slow in its development, despite the spectacular progress of Singapore and Penang as important trading centres in the region – they soon became the main entrepôt or free trade exchange centres of South East Asia. The development was hampered by the factors already mentioned – mountainous terrain with difficult communications, small but fiercely independent native States, and hence the lack of any great economic resources to stimulate trade. The primitive conditions hampered the tin industry, which later made enormous advances under British administration.

Contact between the British colony of the Straits Settlements and the Malay States developed in various ways. First, trade with the outside world was carried on by the Malay States, as it was by much of South East Asia, through Singapore particularly, but Penang always remained an important port. The colony was a base from which British and other travellers and explorers began their journeys into the Peninsula, as well as into Siam and the Eastern Archipelago, and the writings of these travellers remain as the main source of modern knowledge of conditions in the countries they described.

Many of the Chinese concerned in the tin industry, and most of those who gained ownership of the individual mines, were resident in the British colony and therefore British subjects. Sometimes the miners were molested, even killed, in the sporadic lawlessness in the Malay States, which of course gave rise to demands for British protection and intervention. The troubles of the tin industry actually gave the immediate initiative for British official concern. In 1874, the Sultan of Perak agreed to accept a 'British Resident' as his adviser in government, and soon after the Sultan of Selangor, where Kuala Lumpur is situated, followed suit. Conditions existing at the time may be gauged by noting that the first British Resident to Perak was murdered soon after his arrival, apparently due to faction fighting among Malay groups.

The adjoining States, Pahang and Negeri Sembilan, made similar agreements and in 1896 all four States were combined in the Federated Malay States which had a federal government with control over matters of common interest, finance, taxation, police, customs and posts, later railways and telegraphs. The State Councils continued to deal with matters of local interest, such as health, education and land regulation, but all followed agreed principles and standards inspired by the federal government, which was a British creation. In about 20 years, at the outbreak of the First World War, services and conditions in the Federated Malay States were comparable with those developed in the Straits Settlements.

An important reason for this rapid advance was the unification of the Colonial Service throughout the Empire under the Colonial Office, London, whose head was the member of the British Government holding the post of Secretary of State for Colonies. The government officers serving in the Malay States varied their service with that in the Straits Settlements, and of course it was the experience derived from a century's development in the Settlements which was immediately available for the Malay States. All the territories are adjacent and hence have the same climate, land environment and population composition – Malays, Chinese and Indians with small additions from much of Asia, from the Arabs of the Hadramaut in South Arabia to the Filipinos. However, the *proportions* of the races in each territory vary, for example mostly Chinese in Singapore, mostly Malays in Kelantan. This kind of development is only possible on a comprehensive scale in an Empire administration where readily available and easy migration from one area to another is possible (see Appendix 1).

Empires have both their positive uses and advantages, which comprise their permanent contribution to civilisation. Those who underwent a classical education, as did I, will know that the Roman Empire derived much of its strength from its civil service, some of whose officials have their careers recorded in some detail (e.g. Agricola in Britain, the Younger Pliny in the Middle East).

It was important for British officials connected with Malaya to have regard to the influence of Siam, now Thailand. The northern Malay States, Kedah, Perlis, Kelantan and Trengganu, were under the hegemony of Siam, which was of course mainly concerned with their contacts with foreign powers. Thus the sale by the Sultan of Kedah in 1786 to the British of Province Wellesley, the strip of territory opposite Penang Island, caused considerable argument for long afterwards with the Siamese Government. It is obvious that the interests of these four States are much closer to those of the southern States than with those in the north in Siam, so in 1909 Britain arranged a treaty with Siam that the four States should be British Protectorates. Thus the situation until the Japanese invasion in 1942 was that the nine Malay States were divided into the four Federated Malay States and five Unfederated Malay States. Johore signed an agreement for British protection in 1914, but was averse to joining the Federated States, despite its position between Singapore and the Federated States. Thus the Malayan railway, which ran from Singapore to the Siam border, and then straight through to Bangkok in the Siam railway system, was the 'Johore State railway' when it passed through Johore.

In brief, British administration created Malaya as a united economic and political identity. The tin industry, as stated earlier a Chinese exploit for some centuries, was rapidly developed by an influx of British capital and engineering technology. Much of the tin ore was retrieved from river banks, and the huge dredges used for this purpose became a common feature in the Federated Malay States. These dredges originated from a similar situation in New Zealand, where they had been used to dredge gold from river beds. The topography, forest vegetation and wet climate of the two countries are very similar, and made me feel 'very much at home' during my time in Malaya.

The rubber industry was a British creation. From rubber seeds smuggled out of Brazil, their native habitat, to the Royal Botanic Gardens at Kew, London, seeds were produced of which some were sent in 1877 to the Singapore Botanic Gardens. The Gardens acted as a nursery for supply to estates, not only in Malaya but ultimately throughout South East Asia, to Indonesia, Ceylon, Indochina and Thailand. The rubber tree soon proved to be very adaptable to the Malayan climate, but there was little demand for rubber until the automobile industry developed after 1900.

The supply of Brazilian natural rubber, derived from the country's jungles, proved unable to meet the demand, which resulted in a great expansion of rubber estates in Malaya, founded by British companies. By 1914 the output of estate rubber exceeded that of Brazilian jungle rubber, and by 1920 Malaya was producing 53 per cent of world production. As well as the British estates, Chinese and Malay smallholders also joined in the production, and contributed about 40 per cent to the Malayan market. The result was to make Malaya the most prosperous unit of the British Empire; that is, of the colonies controlled by the Colonial Office. Singapore and Penang received great benefit, as the rubber was exported and sold through these ports.

For the purposes of this memoir, three aspects of Malayan development between the two world wars are of special importance. First, the economic advances deriving from the tin and rubber industries enabled rapid improvements in the government services, in all fields. In education, a complex and efficient system, consisting of English-medium, Malay, Chinese and Indian (usually Tamil) schools, was developed, which consistently drew upon contemporary advances in curriculum and school organisation, especially in Britain and other Empire countries.

Science was introduced in English schools, which in fact kept up to the standard of the best schools overseas. The University of Cambridge Examinations Syndicate set the school leaving examinations throughout the entire Colonial Empire, and these certificates were in all respects equivalent to those granted in Britain. Hence they gave admission to universities, professional training or clerical employment wherever British qualifications were accepted. Physical training and the standard school sports were usual in English schools and increasingly in others, and special schools such as trade, commercial and agricultural schools were established.

Second, there had been a slow development in providing formal, that is school, education for girls. None of the races had any tradition of providing this type of education, and even in the Straits Settlements there was little progress in establishing girls' schools before 1900. The majority of the girls' English schools were the creation of various church missionary organisations, first the Anglican, but by far the majority were run by Catholics, especially the Convent of the Holy Infant Jesus (Dames de St Maur), and the American Episcopal Methodist Mission. Men's missionary orders in these churches also made an important contribution to the boys' schools.

In Perak and Selangor, girls' English schools were developed from the 1920s onwards, and some of the original missionary teachers were still serving in the schools in 1946. They used to tell me how in the early years they had to knock on the doors of merchants and professional people, begging them to send their daughters to school. For some years the girls were conducted from home to school in closed carriages, then in rickshaws and latterly accompanied by servants. This was purely a matter of custom, since until the Japanese invasion, Malaya was one of the most peaceful and law-abiding countries in the world.

The previous account applies only to the Chinese and Indian communities; in the Muslim tradition, to different degrees, girls are segregated, and there was active opposition to Malay girls attending school at all. After the First World War, education for Malay boys, which originally was also opposed, had developed to the extent that primary education was compulsory in every State. But education for Malay girls was instituted only between the wars, and did not begin to be much accepted until a few years before Japanese occupation. At this time, a curriculum on the same lines as that in the boys' schools slowly developed, differentiated by the inclusion of needlework and domestic science in some schools.

At the outbreak of war, enrolment in the Malay girls' schools totalled only a third of that of the boys' schools, which meant that in the more remote parts of the country Malay girls' schools did not exist.

The third point is really a summing up of the preceding account. In most aspects of government activity, considerable progress had been made and, especially in the towns, facilities – housing, health, communications – were of a high standard. Accordingly, services and amenities varied a great deal over the whole country. For example, it was estimated that only half the total of Chinese children attended school at all, and of these most were boys. Therefore, the proportion of Chinese girls attending school in 1941 would be no higher than that of Malay girls. This point is emphasised here because it is the essential basis of what follows.

In my time in post-war Malaya, developments were still possible by building on the foundations laid by previous generations, even if these had been greatly negated by the privations and suffering endured during the Japanese occupation. As will be generally known, much post-war commentary concerning the British Empire in all its aspects was negative and adversely critical, and at times antagonistic. The general underlying theme of the criticism was that progress under British rule could have been faster and more all-embracing. As indicated above, in my view this criticism has no basis in fact or in history, and the developments made during the period of British rule often suffered from contemporary criticism, which considered such changes as too sudden and imposed by a western civilisation against the interests and desires of Asians. The latter is, in my opinion, a more accurate perspective.

The change in conditions post-war was nothing less than a revolution from the pre-war situation. A factor in this change was the increasing tendency of Chinese and Indians to make their homes in Malaya, instead of being temporary employees in tin-mines, shops or rubber estates. For centuries there had always been a few Indian and Chinese traders resident in Malayan ports, but the development of industries in the twentieth century caused a rapid increase in the permanently resident non-Malay population (that is both Chinese and Indians together), estimated to be about 50 per cent of the total population. Of course the post-war conditions in both India, following independence in 1947, and China, after the Communist assumption of power in 1949, caused an increased trend towards permanent Malayan residence by the non-Malay population, which was an important factor in the politics and negotiations leading to independence in 1957.

Chapter 1
Early life

The Colonial Service was a British Government institution, and applicants were required to have been born in the British Isles, i.e. in the United Kingdom, or in the Republic of Ireland whose citizens had equal opportunities to those of British birth. From the mid-1920s a new departure was to open the Service to citizens of the 'Dominions' – Canada, Australia, New Zealand, South Africa and some smaller countries such as Newfoundland and Southern Rhodesia. Qualifications, training and experience were in all respects similar to those required of British entrants, and indeed the same application forms were used as for British applicants.

I was born in Auckland in the suburb of Otahuhu on 29 November 1913. My father, Thomas Taylor, born in Manchester, arrived in New Zealand as an 'assisted immigrant' in 1904, and spent his early years in New Zealand in Greymouth on the west coast of the South Island. My mother, Nellie Warren, was the fifth of nine children of assisted immigrants who had arrived from Devon in 1874. She had qualified as a pupil teacher to teach in primary schools. At the time of her marriage in 1912, she was the infant mistress at the large Greymouth District High School, in charge of the primer classes. These were attended by children of five years of age for about two years from their admission before entering the 'Standards', six progressive classes until the primary school leaving age of about 13 years. The infant mistress was in fact the senior woman assistant in a primary school and hence enjoyed the highest salary for primary school women teachers. There were no teachers' colleges in New Zealand until 1906.

Before leaving England my father had supplemented his primary education by attending evening classes at the university, which of course advanced the students' education but did not lead to a degree. Thus his general education was judged sufficient to teach in a primary school, and he was given a year's training in Auckland primary schools. The next year, 1914, he was given a single-teacher country school in a remote district in Taranaki in the centre of the North

Island. Three years later he was moved to a two-teacher school, still in Taranaki, in the small country village of Whangamomona, on the railway line 40 miles east of Stratford. This line was being built through mountainous country to connect with the main Auckland–Wellington railway, which was achieved in 1933.

The other teacher in the school of about seventy pupils was a woman teacher who taught the lower classes, and here I received all my primary school education. The township had one street, which contained a post office, bank, grocer, draper, butcher, baker, licensed hotel and blacksmith, and later a garage. In the 1920s, motor cars gradually made their appearance, tractors replaced horses on the farms and small trucks instead of horse-drawn carts transported farm products and brought in supplies.

My school days were undistinguished except for two things. I read early and soon became an omnivorous reader, which was just as well because I was subject to bronchitis, and later bronchial catarrh, up until the time I had completed university, a year at teachers' college and the next year's practical training as a probationary assistant. The doctors said I would 'grow out of it', but in the primary school I spent several weeks each winter in bed, being treated with 'inhalations'. Subsequently I was rarely absent from classes, but in the winter months I often experienced congestion of the lungs. I managed to turn out for the usual school games most of the time – in New Zealand, rugby and cricket – but without any marked ability in either. I have been short-sighted from birth; my susceptibility to bronchial asthma was a handicap, but my working life was free of almost any ailment – a happy contrast.

Secondary education was free of school fees for all pupils who passed the top class in primary schools,[5] when a Proficiency Certificate was issued. A class examination was held in the schools each year by the school inspectors. However, as much of the population lived on small farms, the countryside was dotted with small villages and towns, with a few large towns, known as 'provincial centres', where local industries, government administration and the large secondary schools were situated. So the problem for country parents who wished to send their promising sons and daughters to high school was not to pay fees, but to pay the cost of boarding at the school hostels, which were almost always attached to the large secondary schools.

Accordingly, the Education Department provided secondary school scholarships, the junior scholarship for pupils leaving primary school, and the senior at third year in the secondary school, each tenable for three years. The scholarships provided a small amount towards the cost of school books (£5 and £10), but for pupils boarding at secondary school there was sufficient to pay board at a school hostel (£40 and £60). The latter amount was the same as that paid for university scholarships. These scholarships in succession provided the means for bright country students to go through to university. I succeeded in obtaining both the junior and senior scholarships, but as I was due to go to secondary school, my father was transferred to a small school near Stratford which had a small high school but no hostel. As the distance to Stratford was only four miles by train, I did not need to use the boarding allowances. Two years after gaining the senior scholarship, I gained a Taranaki provincial scholarship to the university.

During my second year at high school, the chairman of the high school board gave his private library to the school. These volumes took up the space round the walls of one classroom and consisted of works of classical English literature, art books of the old masters and a wide range of history. This fortunate event of course ensured that when I went up to university my reading was wider than most of my contemporaries. I recollect that, strangely, there was in the library a fairly recent Colonial Office List setting out the posts in each Territory which were staffed by Colonial Service Officers. I had never considered any career other than teaching, and took special note of the positions in education. These varied in number and salary, of course, according to the size and resources of the Territory, and one I remember was Aden, where the only Colonial Service post in education was the director! There was then no anticipation that 20 years later I should take up one of these positions.

It has always puzzled me that school libraries should so slowly have been recognised as an essential facility at every level. It is well known, and often emphasised by educational writers, that reading is an essential factor for progress in English language learning. High school staffs used to comment that they could always tell the primary schools that had library facilities.

In my time at school, in country districts there would only be a few dozen pupils, from families of lawyers, doctors and teachers, and other professional people, who had any books at all at home. My father was himself widely read and a good teacher, and a good collection of literature at home was obviously a great advantage to me throughout my school years. There was always a collection of suitable books in the schools in which my father taught. In most farmers' homes, owing to the poor communications in country districts, not even the daily newspaper was seen. The *Taranaki Herald* used to issue a weekly news digest, the *Taranaki*

Budget, which was the only printed matter in the home other than the Bible and the children's textbooks. Hence the enormous value of a good reading collection available at school for taking home.

The official qualification for entry to the university was the matriculation examination, at the fourth year of high school. This was sometimes passed by brighter students at third year, which I managed, followed by a Taranaki university scholarship the following year. This surprised everyone, including myself, as university scholarships were usually attained in the fifth year at high school. The decision (mainly my mother's) was therefore to send me up to Auckland the following year.

There really was no other choice; it was indeed a case of 'now or never', and as will be seen later, history has only confirmed the wisdom of this decision. Of course, the reason was the onset of the Great Depression which struck New Zealand in 1930. To give an example, in 1929, the price of wool per pound was 21 pence (a very good return). In 1930 the price was only 10 pence, and the following year, 1931, 4½ pence, at which level wool prices remained for three years.

Of my sixth-form classmates in 1930, two girls went to Otago University in Dunedin, and a number of girls went to Auckland Teachers' College, while the other two boys obtained posts in the Public Service in Wellington. The sudden onset of the Depression caused the government to reduce expenditure drastically, with even the appearance of panic. The teachers' colleges were to close, the 1931 students would complete their course in 1932, and there were no further intakes until 1935. When the students left college, almost all joined the unemployed, which of course was the fate of their predecessors the previous year, and indeed also of most university graduates. As a relief measure, the government arranged for the unemployed teachers to be attached to schools near their homes, and to be paid a small allowance similar to a scholarship grant. This at least maintained morale, and ensured that the teachers would maintain their skills and be able to resume employment easily when required.

On my arrival in Auckland in March 1931, there was no doubt that economic conditions were grim. The situation was made obvious by a closed newspaper office (*The Sun*), a large amusement park closed and deserted, and already there were empty shops in suburban streets. Unemployment was already higher than in living memory, and hastily organised relief agencies were endeavouring to give aid in clothing and food. Actually, New Zealand had had little unemployment since the 1880s, so that there was no prepared government relief organisation. Parliament was called and immediately approved a special relief tax of sixpence in the pound, the next year raised to two shillings, at which it remained for the next few years. Salaries and wages were reduced by degrees down by 20 per cent, and government charges – railway fares and freight, and postages – heavily reduced.

In the university, most students struggled to pay their fees, and find money for board and food. We walked where possible to save tram fares. Social life became very informal – the customary balls and formal dances were foregone and social efforts were confined to the usual observance of the graduation ceremony and the ensuing dance. My memory is that despite the parsimony, students generally took the view that they were lucky to be studying and fortunate to be doing something positive towards qualifying for a career when times improved. In fact, university enrolments soon increased to rather more than they had been before the Depression.

My choice of Auckland University College owed its initiative to the availability of a university hostel for men, and to the presence in the city of two aunts and two uncles. For some reason unknown to me, obtaining board in any of the main cities was always difficult, and a major problem for young people coming to the city for study or employment – more so for the women than the men. The teachers' colleges in each of the main centres – Auckland, Wellington, Christchurch and Dunedin – provided women's hostels. As most of the students in Dunedin came from elsewhere to study in the specialist schools – medicine, dentistry, home science, physical education, etc. – the provision of boarding was much more adequate, as perforce the university for most of its history was, and still is, the major economic support of the city. As the original university (1868), it developed the full range of faculties early. The university colleges established in Christchurch (1872), Auckland (1886) and Wellington (1898) developed as liberal arts colleges in the faculties of Arts, Science, Law and Commerce, with one or two additions. Christchurch has the main School of Engineering.

When I completed the four-year Arts degree course in 1934, I was fortunate to be admitted to the one-year Graduate course in Auckland Teachers' College when it reopened in 1935, and began teaching the following year. The aim of the Graduate course was to train secondary school teachers, and students spent half the time in teaching practice in the schools – secondary schools, a technical college, a junior high school (in New Zealand now called intermediate schools) – which usually began with a primary school class to gain some acquaintance with the life of the children before they advanced to secondary school. A total of six classes in separate schools was visited by each student, two schools each term, spending about six weeks in each.

Male students were required to do at least two primary school practices, including one with young children. This was because the number of positions in boys' secondary schools was relatively small, and men once appointed usually spent their entire career in the one school, unless they secured an appointment as principal. Hence the turnover of staffs at boys' secondary schools was very slow, and some years' service in primary schools was inevitable. In contrast, it was still usual for female teachers to resign on marriage, so even the smaller girls' high schools would usually have two or three vacancies each year. My graduate class at teachers' college numbered about thirty, about half men and half women, and from memory most of the women had obtained positions in the next year (1936) or so. Some of the men, who had attended the larger schools, were also appointed to their 'old schools', but most of us on average had to wait three years or more. I may add that we spent the time applying for suitable positions, and achieved considerable expertise in framing our applications and the accompanying CVs (curriculum vitaes). In fact, I had over four years' primary school experience, teaching all classes from the 5-year-old entrants to the top Proficiency Certificate classes, preparing pupils to enter secondary school the following year.

In the event, my entry to a secondary school staff was hastened by the outbreak of war. In New Zealand, secondary schools had units of school cadets, and masters were commissioned in the Territorial Army, of which the school cadets were the junior branch. Hence, when the war began, these high school cadet officers provided a readily available supply of officers for the hastily assembled New Zealand Expeditionary Force (NZEF), a difficult task after the years of low expenditure on the armed services, their training and equipment. The NZEF was formed in three sections in 1939–1940 and despatched to Egypt as each section (echelon) was ready.

New Zealand, as in the First World War, adopted conscription early in the Second World War, which meant that men of military age were given medical examinations, and progressively called up by ballot as required. In certain occupations, such as teaching, men were retained in employment for some time; the aim was to ensure the minimum dislocation in the schools following the departure of those required immediately for military service.

When the Japanese attacked Pearl Harbor in December 1941, the conditions and outlook in New Zealand changed literally overnight. Every able-bodied man who could possibly be spared from essential work was called up, and the country placed on an active war footing. Thus I entered a military camp in January 1942 along with contemporaries from various occupations, who until then had been retained in civilian employment as 'essential workers'. The contingency was apparent that Australia and New Zealand might have to face a Japanese invasion, of what dimensions no one could guess. Singapore fell on the 15 February 1942, and the situation was very critical until the defeat of the Japanese at the Battle of Midway in June 1942.

Chapter 2

Retrospect: a historical review

When news broke of the bombing of Pearl Harbor and the Japanese invasion of Malaya early in December 1941, the staffs of schools were busy marking end of year examination papers. As I never returned to civilian employment in New Zealand, the end of the school year and entry into military service was a major event in my life, perhaps the most important.

A glance at the changes which have taken place in the lifetime of recent generations may help to give some perspective; most people are aware of the continuous and rapid changes which mark recent history, but it is not so generally realised that the conditions are unique. There was felt to be a void of sympathy between my generation and the next, and most people will be aware of the term 'generation gap' coined to express the situation.

Perhaps the differences between the last two generations were more marked than any previously; this, in my opinion, was the culmination of at least four generation gaps. These included developments back to the period of colonisation in the latter part of the nineteenth century. It has been noted by social historians that the condition of the common people did not change much in essence over the centuries following Roman times. One generation followed another, children having no expectation for their future other than that it would be very similar to that of their parents. Any improvement in the human condition was dependent on ability and industry, and of course most importantly the bounty of the seasons. Most of the population, directly or indirectly, were dependent on the annual harvests. There was no transport, except by horse, which could only be afforded by the wealthy, or used by tradesmen to convey their products from source to shops. The vast majority of people lived and died within ten miles of where they were born – that is, within walking distance for an able-bodied adult.

All this changed about the middle of the nineteenth century, due to the invention of the steam locomotive and the advent of the railways. By about 1860 railways had been extended over the populous parts of Britain, and ordinary working people could travel cheaply anywhere in the country. Of course, young people tried their fortunes in the large cities, especially London. At the same time, ocean transport became safer, and in favourable conditions even provided some comfort, first with the larger sailing vessels, and later in the century with steamships. Emigration across the seas to North America, and even on the longer voyages to Australia and New Zealand, could be readily contemplated by women and by parents of young families, the main hazard being shipwreck on the treacherous and little known coasts near their final destination. The first generation gap was therefore a result of emigration, which brought challenges quite different from those common in the 'home country'.

The gold rushes in the 1850s and 1860s to Victoria, New South Wales and Queensland were made possible by the improved transport by sea. Taking 1850 as a median point for the next generation, the struggle to establish homes, farms and businesses entailed long working hours and much hardship, which was partly due to the lack of transport from the ports to the inland settled areas. The limitation of resources, including food, meant that strict domestic discipline was essential. Gradually the hard work produced results in the establishment of industries and hence in much improved economic conditions.

The early years of the twentieth century were remembered by the young generation as a 'golden age' of prosperity and peaceful development. My parents belonged to this generation, my mother being born in 1883. Her parents brought up a family of nine on a small wage, which meant that strict discipline to ensure that not a penny was wasted was essential. In my experience, the generation gap between my parents' generation and their parents was absolute – in my parents view they were brought up too strictly, and this was the common attitude which I recollect in conversation between members of this age group. I stress 'in my experience', because at the same time it was the great age of children's literature with such writers as James Barrie and Rudyard Kipling; but life in the colonies was no doubt harsher than with the middle class at home. The colonials had the advantage that their material prosperity was greater than they could have expected in England; my grandfather (maternal) and father were quite definite in their belief that they did much better in New Zealand than they would have done by staying in their home country.

Taking my generation, born about the time of the First World War, the attitude between us and our parents was curious.

Antagonism, much less violence, was rare but our parents seemed to be unwilling to discuss matters in depth. Though my parents were well read, they did not seem to be interested in the books I was reading – much of it by the usual classical English authors, Chaucer, Shakespeare and later writers. Their formal education was of only primary school standard, and it may have been a lack of confidence that prevented them from contributing to discussion. I gathered that the situation with many families of my contemporaries was similar – parents were pleased when we succeeded and were proud of our achievements – but our pursuits were not within their area of understanding.

The next generation is of course that of our children, born after the 1940s (now dubbed the 'baby boomers') and advancing now into positions of importance and responsibility. In Australia, high schools were built very rapidly after the Second World War, the aim being to allow every child the chance of a secondary education. In Perth there were high schools in every suburb, with enrolments of a thousand or more. Pre-war there were only three state high schools in Perth, a 'selective' school for intending university students, a boys' and a girls' school, and mixed high schools in the five country towns, all small. The private schools had more secondary classes, but many pupils, even from the wealthier homes, left in their third year. For a girl to complete a secondary course was uncommon, and for her to go to university was even rarer. So most students going to university in the 1960s and 1970s had parents who had not advanced beyond the primary school.

All of this means that the traditions handed down from one generation to another have not only been broken, but in many quarters have entirely dissipated. A previously unheard of phenomenon nowadays is the proliferation of 'codes of ethics' for teachers, librarians, doctors, accountants, banks, businesses – and others. Reasonably well-nurtured families in the past would be familiar with the Bible, often read daily at home, and expounded each Sunday in church. Apart from the specific religious teaching, the Bible describes and explains human character expressed in daily action, and these characters formed the basis of discussion or of sermons. Those who studied the Greek and Latin classics had reinforcement from those literatures – for centuries able writers have commented on the actions of the Greek wars, of Julius Caesar, Augustus, Mark Anthony, and so on, and this discussion still continues. The result was that ordinary people, let alone the educated, were used to assessing character and conduct from infancy, and had a sound basis, well used in practice, for judging what was right, or reasonable, or kindly in their own daily work and behaviour. (No criticism is intended concerning these codes of ethics as such; previous generations would just not have understood the need for them.) Codes of ethics, of necessity, omit the most important thing – no code can prescribe the action or conduct which is best in any given situation. Civilised behaviour does not depend on learning a set of rules, but in training and practice in assessing situations and making decisions appropriate to all the relevant factors, for which experience and education are essential.

Another phenomenon, well known to staffs of academic institutions, and sometimes to percipient parents, is the marked change in attitude which can take effect from one year's entry of students to the next, and in the twentieth century usually in periods of three to five years at most. Reference has already been made to the Depression which struck New Zealand in the 1930s, with a sudden onset in 1931. Students then in their third or fourth year (the usual length of an Arts or Science course), wondered where they were and what had struck them. Generally, teachers did not lose their jobs during the Depression in New Zealand, so those who had gained appointments by 1930 were not personally greatly affected. However, those completing qualifications in later years, as mentioned earlier, had several years of unemployment, ameliorated by makeshift arrangements. Taking the age of 20 as the point of comparison, there would be at least ten well-marked successive age groups in this century, each with different ideologies and social attitudes. No wonder children and parents 30 years or so apart often do not understand each other. Real effort by those concerned is necessary to achieve a viable, let alone a happy relationship. As suggested earlier, this problem is a unique occurrence in the last century or so.

Chapter 3
War service, 1942–1946

When I returned home for Christmas in 1941 there was waiting an official envelope which instructed me to report at the army office in Wellington regarding a posting. This in itself was unusual, as the notices generally gave instructions to report to a stated unit in a training camp. When I duly appeared at the office, I was greeted by the posting officer with 'Well, you have a good job: you are to join the reinforcement of the Pacific Islands Force [always shortened to PIF] and go to Fanning Island in a few weeks.'

Fanning Island is an isolated atoll in the middle of the Pacific, about 1,500 kilometres from Honolulu. Accordingly, I reported to Trentham Military Camp, Wellington, on 10 January 1942, and was assigned to a 'hut' containing about thirty men posted to the same unit. As most people with military experience or students of war history are aware, the capital problem is to keep troops occupied, especially during long periods of inactivity. Fanning Island was a cable station on the British cable route across the Pacific from Canada to Australia and New Zealand. It was essential that troops posted to the island had to be managed without entertainment facilities. They had to be able to while away time by reading or playing cards, chess, darts and such, as well as be able to endure each other's company for months, much like an Antarctic expedition. We were mostly in our late twenties, all had had responsible positions in various occupations, mainly professional, and I doubt whether there was any man in the group without a university degree. We had barely got acquainted when the news arrived that the PIF was abolished, as the Americans had taken control of the island.

When war broke out in 1939, New Zealand assumed responsibility for the defence of the Pacific Islands of the British Empire, including Fiji, and at the same time maintained a division in the Middle East which continued until the end of the war. It was quite clear that events overseas were moving quickly, as there were changes in the disposition of the units in training every week or two. Our intake, like our predecessors, would have formed another reinforcement for the Middle East, but after the Japanese entry into the war the immediate concern was home defence. It appeared that our unit would become a trained reserve in case of an invasion, while providing as much help as possible for the protection of the islands to the north. The normal recruit training period was reduced to an intensive minimum, with the aim of creating an immediately useful force. As soon as training began, we were given the essential minimum of drill, and immediately given weapon training and practice on the range.

Singapore fell on the 15th of February, and the Americans made enormous efforts to recover from Pearl Harbor, their advance across the Pacific being quite remarkable. As stated above, the Americans had taken over Fanning Island by the middle of January and after the PIF was scrapped, I must have been posted around Trentham Camp successively to about five different units as dispositions were redrawn following the trend of events. Finally, I was posted to the field artillery, and after one week's experience in handling the guns, we were given a few days' 'final leave' and embarked from Auckland on a Royal Navy reserve ship HMS *Ascania*, which was a converted Canadian emigrant ship. We left Auckland on 19 April 1942 and reached Suva without incident four days later.

To give some impressions of my recruit training, I knew my way round Trentham Camp, as I had had some experience as a school cadet in two summer camps where boys, selected as NCOs, were sent for a week during the summer holidays. Trentham Camp had been one of them. The recreation facilities were immeasurably better, as were the newer huts compared with the First World War buildings, some of which were still in use. In the latter, ablutions had to be performed in the open with tin basins, with water drawn from taps fitted along benches. The modern buildings had all facilities under cover.

The recreation facilities were provided by various welfare organisations of the churches. My recollection is that in my visits in 1928 and 1929 the only hut was that of the Salvation Army, but in 1942 there were about six, which included huts provided by the Anglican and Catholic Churches. The buildings in every organisation were similar, quite spacious and comfortable, and they provided a canteen supplying hot and cold drinks and meals. The leisure facilities included billiards, darts, chess and draughts and a reading and writing room (stationery supplied).

First World War veterans, who for the most part constituted the camp officers, warrant officers and the clerical and maintenance staff, thought we were being brought up in the lap of luxury. The reason for the provision of these facilities was the view that in an emergency (e.g. a Japanese invasion), leave might be stopped for an indefinite period, during which the facilities in the camps would provide sufficient relief from army routine. This contingency, of course, never occurred, but I can vouch for the high standard of the services provided by very pleasant people, male and female, most of whom were voluntary workers. Alcoholic beverages, I should add, were provided only in one place, the camp canteen, open at restricted times and always under strict surveillance. The latter was necessary because from time to time there had been mayhem on the final night in camp before a unit's embarkation, indeed it was said that every glass in the canteen was smashed on one such night. Our artillery reinforcement of about 120 of all ranks left Trentham railway station, farewelled by the camp military band to the NZEF tune 'We are the boys from way down under', for the long railway journey to Auckland, about 450 miles, and embarkation.

Our arrival in Suva, capital of Fiji, on the south-east of the main island, Viti Levu, was during the wet season. This island is surrounded by a coral reef which has two gaps, one opposite Suva, the other opposite Lautoka, on the other side of the island, which is roughly circular in shape. At this latitude, 18 ° S, the prevailing wind is easterly, which means that the eastern side of the island gets a heavy tropical rainfall. As the interior contains high mountains, the western side has a much drier climate. The first experience of this climate is to make you think you have been placed in a perpetual steam bath, which in our two weeks there did not change much at night. It also gave me an example of the strange effects the tropics can have on people from the temperate regions; within the two weeks, two of our number of about 120 returned sick to Auckland on the ship which had brought us to Suva.

We travelled to Lautoka on the deck of a cargo ship which took about a day to make the journey. It was quite an experience to sleep in the open in the tropics at night, with a pleasant warm atmosphere. It transpired on our arrival that the assignment of the field regiment was to ensure that no enemy craft, surface or submarine, could pass through the gap in the reef opposite the port of Lautoka. For this purpose all the batteries were placed on hills overlooking the harbour (the Nadi, pronounced 'Nandi', airport was just below us) and our tents were placed close to the guns of our battery.

A regiment of artillery is equivalent in status to a battalion of infantry, which is divided into companies; the batteries were the components of the artillery regiment, and ours had distinct types of guns in each battery, from those used in the First World War to the latest, the 'twenty-five pounder'. Consequently, our few months in Fiji were spent digging gun pits.

At the weekends we were allowed to go to Lautoka on leave; there was no regular transport, so you either walked, which I did, or thumbed a ride with army transport on duty. In Fiji, the large towns, Suva and Lautoka, were mainly Indian in population; the native Fijians lived in villages dotted all over the island. My recollection is the frequency with which one heard continual sounds of laughter and enjoyment as one passed a Fijian village; in the town of Lautoka crying children were almost as common. It was a contrast between two civilisations, not merely of two races. The Indians had been brought to Fiji to work the sugar plantations, as had the Malaya Indians who came to work on rubber estates; this was done for the same reason – the native people were not interested in regular daily employment of fixed hours. The problem was that the Indians grew in number to equal the Fijian population, which has caused racial and constitutional difficulties up to the present time.

My first stay in the tropics accordingly passed very happily; the only drawback was that it was so brief. Only two occurrences are worthy of mention. Before we left New Zealand, there had only been time to give us the first of two injections against tropical diseases, and the second was administered soon after our arrival above Nadi. For good measure, we had vaccinations as well. The day after we had the inoculations, the colonel decided to test the guns for range and efficiency (called 'calibration') and many of us had high temperatures – the combined effects of the inoculations and the unusual climate. So following a sick parade, those of us who reported ill were allowed to lie down in our tents, which of course were quite close to the gun sites; every time the guns fired, we felt as if the tops of our heads were lifting off!

After a few weeks we learnt that the Americans were arriving – this was only June 1942, and we admired their wonderful equipment of every kind, including a complete field hospital. But oddly enough, the Americans lacked the only medication that was absolutely essential – the green paint that was used to check tinea in the feet (athlete's foot) which almost all personnel contracted in that humid climate. So the New Zealand Medical Services stepped into the breach and relieved the Americans. Our only medical trouble was a mysterious tropical fever which had most men confined to bed for a few days. The few of us who were well, of whom I was one, were employed full time preparing meals and carrying them round to those troops who were still interested in eating. This was an indication to me that a career in the tropics might be a possibility.

The main lesson as far as I was concerned was the tropics' ability to 'play tricks' with one's physique – I arrived in Fiji under 12 stone, and left at 15 stone. The excess weight disappeared after my return to New Zealand.

Soon after, word got round that the Americans were taking over the defence of Fiji, and the New Zealanders would return home, in a progressive roster. As the Americans had superior modern weapons, the artillery was placed in the first homebound contingent; this time we were taken round to Suva by the coastal road in army transport – a delightful trip. Our ship was the *President Coolidge*, converted into a troopship to take several thousand men. It did the journey to Auckland in about three days, which were quite uneventful. The Americans catered for meals on a twice daily roster; units being rostered to go to the dining areas from about 8 a.m. onwards. Those on the early morning rosters returned for dinner early in the afternoons in the same order at about six hour intervals, similar to the morning meal. Each man was given a large tray with each kind of food in a separate compartment, all of it excellent in quality and beautifully cooked.

One tragic event in our Fiji experience: our commander was Major General O.H. Mead who walked round the ship talking to us before we sailed. I remember him asking us, 'Do you know where you are going?', which was greeted with laughter and suitable comments. The General was to fly from Fiji to New Zealand soon after our departure, but his aircraft never arrived, and a search of the area where the aircraft was last reported was unsuccessful. Major General Mead was the highest ranking New Zealander to lose his life during the war. Later I learnt that the General and his family lived in the suburb near my wife's family, and were well known and liked in the suburb, so that his disappearance was felt as a personal loss by many local residents.

After we disembarked in Auckland, we went by train to the Papakura Military Camp about 30 miles south, where the (Third) Division was to be reformed and trained for active service in the Pacific Islands. One morning I was ordered to appear at the hospital, and as soon as I entered the waiting room everything became clear, as every man present had only one thing in common – we all wore spectacles. One further indication of how precipitate war preparations had been at the onset of the Japanese war was the fact that we were enlisted in the NZEF at all, and even went on active service overseas. If men were otherwise physically fit, they were simply given army spectacles (steel framed) and sent away with all the others.

My belief has always been that if the war had proceeded in a more gradual fashion, those in my situation would probably not have been enlisted at all – teachers were in short supply once the war had proceeded for some months, especially male secondary teachers, as has been noted above. The attitude would have been that a man was doing more valuable work in a school than doing the routine duties which comprised most of home service, essential as of course those duties were.

It was therefore with genuine regret that I left the battery – overall an excellent group of men by any standards, and above the average in general ability. No better comrades could be found anywhere. My next move was to the Coastal Artillery Regiment, which manned the forts on the hills overlooking Wellington Harbour. The personnel was of two kinds: older men like myself, unfit for overseas service, and young fellows aged 18, most fresh from school, who were not eligible for overseas service, which from recollection they were able to undertake at 20.

The duties were extremely routine – daily drill on the guns, including cleaning and maintenance, with other camp duties as required, for instance cookhouse duty. The wooden barracks were new and comfortable, and gave good protection from the interminable winds of Cook Strait. We had our rifles secured by brackets on the wall next to our beds. One morning I woke up to find my rifle on the floor next to my bed. Surprised I asked my neighbour what had happened, as the other rifles appeared to be in their usual places. The young fellow was equally surprised and asked, 'Didn't you hear the earthquake? We made such a noise that we thought you would wake up.'

On the day (2 July 1942) we embarked at Suva to return to Auckland, radio news was received that Wellington had had a severe earthquake, which of course was of concern to the men who came from that area. We found out that no one was seriously injured, but that damage to buildings was considerable, one of them the Wellington town hall. No one could be spared to repair any building not essential for use, so the town hall was shored up with heavy timber and left for the duration of the war. The earthquake, which I did not hear, caused further damage to some weakened buildings, which were demolished and the sites left vacant until peace returned.

In New Zealand the Education Department published the *Education Gazette*, which included advertisements for vacancies in the schools and for other appointments, such as school inspectors. As stated earlier, teachers were employed by Education Boards, to whom applications were sent direct by each applicant, not through the school principal or employing body. The end of year issue usually included lengthy vacancy lists. An additional drain of male teachers from high schools occurred as men were drafted to the RNZAF training establishments as instructors in mathematics and science. Masters taught navigation and elementary mathematics to cadet air crew, competence in these subjects being essential before the cadets were passed out for flying training.

When the Japanese came into the war, one major consideration was to increase the air force units in New Zealand far beyond those required while hostilities were concentrated in Europe and its adjacent areas. The maintenance staff of necessity comprises the bulk of air force personnel, as the aircraft have to be kept as far as possible continuously at maximum standards, day and night. Accordingly, to have available maintenance crews in this way all the time, it is clear that large numbers of trained persons (from the beginning of the war women were included in the WAAF service) were essential. Staff were trained in the 'technical training school' and entrants also had to begin their training with an elementary course in mathematics and physics, adapted to the basic knowledge required for technical courses. These preliminary courses were also taught by education officers obtained from the science staffs of high schools.

And so it happened that a few months after I had entered the Coastal Artillery, there was an advertisement for education officers for the air force, for qualified teachers with experience in secondary schools. It was apparent to me that I was not really fully employed in my situation, so I sent in my application, as directed in the advertisement, to the director of education by the date stated. By way of explanation, the *Education Gazette* was circulated to reading rooms and offices in the services for information about teachers. In a short while I received a summons to appear at the Regimental Headquarters and there was ushered into the office of the colonel (no less). He immediately gave me a 'ticking off' for sending my application direct to the Education Department, instead of through the official channels, which would have been through his office to District Army Headquarters, then to the Education Department.

In civil life, the colonel was a railway official, and he told me that surely in the Education Department applications went through official channels. It took some persuading to put over to him the actual procedure followed by the teaching service – in my short experience I had applied for, and been appointed to, three posts in succession under three separate boards. In the end the interview concluded amicably; I was suitably contrite about my ignorance of official procedure in the services and he agreed to let the application go forward with his approval. Of course if my application had been for a transfer in the army, it would have been first presented to the commanding officer. My recollection is that the advertisement for education officers specified that applications on the usual education forms were to go to the Education Department, there was no mention of other 'official channels'. Also from memory, all the education officers with whom I worked had been recruited direct from the classroom, or in a few cases had been promoted from the ranks while serving in the RNZAF.

April 1943 accordingly saw me, after still another change, in the Officers' School of Instruction in the RNZAF station in Levin, which is about 60 miles north of Wellington, joining an entry totalling about thirty men, who proved a most interesting group. We were all intended for posts in the Administrative and Special Duties branches of the air force. I was one of four education officers, there were about six engineering officers, four intelligence officers, and several administration officers, or station adjutants and accountants, as well as other groups whom I no longer remember. Every member of the course turned up in the uniform of his current service and rank. Quite a number had served as RNZAF officers for years, but had never had a formal course of officer training. They would have been employed as administrative or engineer officers, performed their duties according to regulation as required, and only now could be spared to undergo the course. Most of the members were NCOs in the air force, who had been recommended for promotion. As the RNZAF was moving up the Pacific in conjunction with the offensive against the Japanese in the Pacific Islands, there was a need for intelligence officers, and some officers had transferred from the army to serve in this capacity. My rank was gunner in the artillery, I think I was the only course member who was not an NCO or in higher rank.

Like most similar institutions used for war-time purposes, the buildings had been converted from a school, with living quarters, mess facilities and a small parade ground. As well as being the officers' school, the station also acted as a first training centre for recruits.

The wide range of backgrounds of the course members made for an interesting time of social contacts along with the official instruction. The staff at the school were also interesting. The commandant (squadron leader), a First World War RAF pilot, was a member of a well-known pastoral and political family with distinguished service in several fields. Our squadron leader was a lawyer in civil life and as he was serving in the RAF when it was formed in 1918, and had had wide legal experience, he was a most interesting and able mentor on the customs and organisation of the Service. The flight lieutenant who lectured on air force law and regulations was, of course, a lawyer also, well grounded in his subject and also an interesting presenter. The third staff member was a retired British Army officer, who in the First World War had been assigned as naval officer at Suva, and thence acquired a commission in the Royal Navy. He was now an officer of the RNZAF and told us that he was proud of his good fortune in being commissioned in all three services. His knowledge and experience of service etiquette and the minutiae of regulations and discipline was encyclopaedic, as could be expected. All three instructors were friendly and helpful, and made us all, even the junior member (me!), feel able to raise any question as the classes proceeded.

In the interests of our health as well as of service routine, parade ground drill and physical exercise were not neglected – I think we had a session each day under a drill sergeant, and sometimes we were taken on a route march round some nearby streets. On one occasion our 'flight' met a horse-drawn greengrocer's cart, driven by two Chinese market gardeners (most of this trade in New Zealand is run by Chinese) who were carrying on a voluble conversation in their own language. One of the intelligence officers had been brought up in China and was fluent in this dialect. As we passed the cart, this officer called out a comment to the Chinese in their language. The two gardeners nearly fell off their seat in their astonishment – apart from any other result, any reputation of the Chinese for being impassive in attitude was completely demolished. In our generation, most of us had learnt French, Latin and perhaps German at school, but I doubt whether there were then a score of Anglo-Saxon New Zealanders who knew any Asian language.

We had an examination at the end of the course, and were told our postings, to take effect after a week's leave. Mine was to RNZAF station Masterton on the other side of the island, across some mountain ranges, about 60 miles north of Wellington.

The reason for my posting to Masterton has never been clear to me. It had been a training station for air crew personnel and at one time had been the headquarters of a squadron, which had, I think, been posted overseas shortly before my arrival in May. There were some personnel doing their initial recruit training, and soon after, the station was closed. Anyhow, after about a week I was transferred to the Technical Training School in Rongotai, a Wellington suburb. The airfield, now much enlarged, serves as the Wellington city airport for international and domestic air services. I was to serve with this school for most of the time I remained in the RNZAF.

Rongotai Airport was one of the first airfields established in New Zealand when commercial air services were developed in the 1920s and 1930s. New Zealand celebrated its centenary of the establishment of formal British rule in 1840 at the end of 1939 and continuing into 1940; of course war broke out at this time, but it was decided to proceed with the celebrations as planned. An important project was the Centenary Exhibition on a site adjacent to Rongotai Airport, and as soon as the exhibition closed in May 1940, the buildings were taken over by the RNZAF. One purpose was as headquarters for the technical branch of the air force, of which the Technical Training School (TTS) was an important, indeed essential, part.

The RNZAF had been established as such only about two years before the war, with personnel on secondment from the RAF. An important part of the RAF personnel consisted of technical officers, who organised the TTS, and these officers were still in charge of the school when I arrived in May 1943. There were a large number of trades in the air force, those with the largest number of personnel being the mechanics and riggers, who between them maintained the engines and the bodies of the aircraft. But there were a large number of smaller trades, for example instrument repairers, whose work was equally important in ensuring the efficient maintenance of the aircraft.

After about six weeks' recruit training in parade ground drill, etc., the recruits did another six weeks' elementary education in mathematics and physics. This consisted of a thorough revision of the 'four rules' in arithmetic (addition, subtraction, multiplication and division) as it was essential that technical staff could calculate quickly and accurately. The rest of the course consisted of elementary mathematics and physics sufficient to enable the airmen to understand the principles of the internal combustion engine, the stresses operating in the fabric of an aircraft and its various parts – wings, tail assembly, etc. Also included were electrical and magnetic fields, conductors and electric circuits, resistances, thermostats, and so on. The recruits had to pass a test in this material before being admitted to the trade courses proper.

Another part of the preliminary training consisted in the use of tools in metal working, practice in filing being an important part. The preliminary section of the TTS was under the charge of a young RAF flight lieutenant, whose staff consisted of education officers to teach the mathematics and physics, and NCOs, sergeants and warrant officers to teach the practical section.

The recruits who had passed the preliminary course were posted to the trade courses in accordance with ability and the preference of the airman, as far as possible. Those with the highest marks in the preliminary test went into the instrument repairing course, where some more advanced mathematical knowledge and the highest standards of accuracy were essential. This course was more demanding, but of course absolute standards of accuracy were emphasised in all the courses.

It should also be explained that these preliminary courses were as important as grading and assessment procedures as much as they were instructional classes. The recruits varied in educational attainment from those who had done a sixth-form course to those who had only passed primary school. The latter found the course very difficult, and it was only the more intelligent and determined who succeeded in meeting the standard set. On the other hand, men who had completed a secondary school course some years before said that they found the course useful as a refresher. We used equipment to illustrate such topics as electric currents, magnetic fields, the working of generators and electric motors, and some men remarked that the equipment made the topics much easier to understand, which had not been the case in their school lessons in the same subjects. Of course we were able to draw upon the assistance of a range of expertise in the TTS staff, and equipment we requested was made in the TTS workshops.

The trainees worked eight hours daily, five days a week; as stated above, half of their time was spent in the classroom and half in the workshop. Each intake was divided into two sections, which alternated between the classroom and the workshop. Thus instruction was carried out continuously during the entire day. Some days education officers taught for the whole eight hours, but on two days we were allowed free periods of half a day when we could go off station. I used some of this time to attend lectures in Greek at the university. My degree contained only one-year's Greek and with the cooperation of the professor and a lecturer, a Fellow of Emmanuel College, Cambridge, 'stranded' in New Zealand when war broke out, I completed the second- and third-year units, which meant I reached final BA standard.

Victoria University College was established in 1899, and the original professors had no retiring age written into their service contracts. The professor must have been about 80 years of age in my time, but still with a very active mind – his exposition of Sophocles' *Antigone* was quite an experience. The lecturer took me through the intricacies of Greek grammar and translation faster than I thought possible, and incidentally I learnt how it was possible to make grammar interesting. I duly passed the examinations each year, which pleased me as ability as a linguist is not really an expertise of mine. During the war I was not required to pay fees – I do not know how many servicemen were able to avail themselves of this opportunity.

As Wellington is the capital, there was a communication flight whose pilots made daily flights delivering mail from and to Air Headquarters in Wellington, and between stations. From memory this service was called the 'milk run', and one pilot, a First World War veteran, lived in our station officers mess and invited me to accompany him when I had a day off duty. I was thus able to see familiar towns from the air, as the aircraft landed frequently. It did not fly at a great height, so this is the only experience I have ever had of actually seeing the surface clearly from the air – you rarely see anything from modern commercial aircraft at cruising altitude. Sadly, I heard later in the war that my pilot was killed when his plane crashed into a mountain during cloudy weather, a tragedy which has occurred to several aircraft in New Zealand, including some passenger planes. I was offered a trip to Norfolk Island, which, though part of Australia, was serviced by the RNZAF. However, we were transferred from Wellington before this flight could take place.

As the war progressed, there were of course changes in the disposition of personnel, units and establishments. After I had been at Rongotai, rumours began to circulate that the TTS was to be moved, and eventually the order came to transfer across Cook Strait to Nelson, a small city in the north of the South Island. The RNZAF station Nelson had previously been a flying station, and had included an air crew training school until shortly before our arrival.

Several things had occurred to change the situation in New Zealand for the RNZAF. By 1944, active hostilities had moved further north and the allies were engaged in 'island hopping', taking one island after another from the Japanese, which meant that New Zealand was no longer a base for operations. The Empire Air Training Scheme in Canada had been in existence for several years, which meant that the air crew training was mainly concentrated in Canada. But the RNZAF was taking an important part in the Pacific war, which meant that the technical services required considerable expansion, hence the importance of the Technical Training School. My guess is that my sudden transfer from Masterton, an air crew training school, to the TTS at Rongotai, marked the change in emphasis to the increase in the provision of technical training.

An air force depends entirely on its aircraft. If for any reason an aircraft is not airworthy, as far as can be ascertained, then it does not fly. And it is the responsibility of many expert and highly trained people to keep the aircraft in a condition of complete readiness. In our course at the school of instruction, the first thing we were told was 'The air force is a technical service', and this of course in no way detracts from the importance of the air crews who fly the aircraft.

An illustration of this last statement occurred to me while I was at Rongotai. From about 1943, servicemen who had spent a specified period on active service – the army in North Africa, the air force over Europe – were progressively returned home to New Zealand, not for demobilisation, but for continued service in less arduous duties. Returning flying personnel were sent to Rongotai station (some may have gone to other stations as well) to await posting to further duties. Of course these young men were keen to get as much flying as possible. One morning at breakfast in the mess, a group of these air crew were loud in their annoyance, because the engineer officer had grounded all the aircraft available for the purposes of a thorough mechanical inspection. The young pilots were highly critical of the engineer officer, and appealed to the commanding officer (CO) of the station. (Station commanders were all qualified pilots.) The CO, of course, upheld his senior engineer with, no doubt, a homily to the effect that if the technical staff do not certify an aircraft as airworthy, no one flies it.

The transfer across Cook Strait went smoothly – there was a great deal of heavy equipment and a multitude of smaller items to be transported – and we were duly installed at RNZAF station Nelson, actually about the same distance from the city as Rongotai is from Wellington city centre. The station was situated near the sea; Rongotai is near the sea and overlooks Cook Strait. But the big difference was that the TTS *was* RNZAF Nelson – there were no other units there, nor any personnel not concerned with the TTS. As I have mentioned, Rongotai was also a flying station, and had responsibility for much else as it was the only station in Wellington, close to Air Headquarters. While at Rongotai, every few weeks I did my turn as station orderly officer, and the number of buildings and security doors we had to check seemed to be simply 'legion'.

To convert the buildings of the flying station at Nelson for use by the TTS proved to be fairly straightforward. The hangars were used as workshops, and the classrooms, formerly used to teach navigation to air crew, were now used to teach physics and mathematics to technical staff. As the TTS numbered far more than the air training school would have done, no doubt additions were made to accommodation, but details of this my memory does not recall. The commandant of the TTS was now the CO of the station, with the usual rank of wing commander.

From the aspect of social life, the change was from the environment of a large city (by New Zealand standards) to a small provincial centre of a population of about 20,000. Wellington is notorious for its climate: the second windiest city in the world, it also has a heavy and continual rainfall, and the climate is unpredictably changeable. Nelson, which its inhabitants delight to call 'Sunny Nelson', has the longest annual tally of hours of sunshine of any city in New Zealand (and there are several others nearly as fortunate), has warm summers and sunny, if rather frosty, winters. The province is perhaps the only area in New Zealand which can be described as having mixed farming – sheep, cattle (dairy and beef), orchards, tobacco, hops, market and flower gardens would not be an exhaustive list – and more of this feature will be described below.

From memory, the total strength of the TTS in our time would be over a thousand, all ranks. This in itself was an important economic boost to Nelson, which for geographic reasons had always been a backwater. Nelson had no rail connection with the rest of the South Island, and road connection was difficult, through mountain passes and over ranges of hills. As already mentioned, though its best land was fertile, it was not extensive in area and none of the industries mentioned was very large. The province had therefore not developed at the same rate as the rest of the country.

A further effect of Nelson's relative stagnation was the large majority of females in the population. In a community where economic activity is not expanding, the young men tend to migrate to areas where there is more employment, which in New Zealand usually meant to Wellington or to Auckland, while for social and other reasons the girls stayed at home. This aspect was brought to my attention at a reception given by the officers' mess soon after our arrival in Nelson. During a discussion some of us had with the mayor, who also represented Nelson in Parliament, he said that the large accession of eligible young men 'would give the girls a chance'. As a matter of fact, many men who did their training in the TTS married Nelson girls and found employment in the district, some of them as farmers, which leads to another story.

As well as teaching educational subjects, mainly mathematics and sciences in the various training courses, education officers also carried out a variety of recreational activities. These might include organising dances and concerts, talks or lectures by visiting speakers on topics of interest to personnel residing on a station, and excursions to places of interest. As noted earlier, Nelson was a small provincial centre, and under war-time conditions did not have a great deal of social attractions. There were about six of us in the education section at Nelson, and it was considered a useful contribution for each education officer to be responsible for one activity. I remember that one of our group was a former New Zealand men's tennis champion, and he put a good deal of life into the station tennis club, and actually organised an open championship tournament one Easter to which townsfolk were invited. It was a great success, both for the tennis competition and socially.

Nelson Province has considerable scenic attractions and also has some features unique in New Zealand, of special interest to those concerned with any of the agricultural industries. By a process of selection, when the various activities were being assigned to members of the education staff, one activity, the Young Farmers' Club, was left unclaimed, and it was given to me, more or less by default, as none of my colleagues had had any contact with farms and agriculture. It so happened that, because I was educated in a country high school, agriculture was one of the sciences which I had taken, along with chemistry. I have always been pleased that this activity fell to my lot. We drew upon the Government Department of Agriculture for instructors in orchards, dairying, sheep, tobacco, hops and apiaries; they were all first class as instructors and we often took air force transport – trucks with temporary seating – on visits to dairy farms, factories, tobacco establishments, and so on. These instructional trips were varied with scenic tours, for which we chartered tourist coaches. The firm of Newmans originated in Nelson, but in due course ran regular bus services in both the South and North Islands, and has now for some years run tours in Australia.

When we first arrived at Nelson, the attendance at meetings was small, only a dozen or so, but soon we were filling two station lorries, and even two coaches, with about sixty persons attending. The girls were encouraged to join in, and we reserved a number of places for the WAAFs which at the beginning did not attract much interest, but before long were oversubscribed. By way of some background information, the Young Farmers' Club had developed into a highly regarded national institution, and when the war began there would be very few districts without a club. They had the full support of the Farmers' Union and the Department of Agriculture, and of course arranged social and sporting activities as well as the scientific lectures and demonstrations.

When the war ended, a survey of the occupations of the personnel was taken before demobilisation, to assist the authorities in providing employment in civilian life. I found out that at the date of the survey, the number of farmers among the station personnel was much less than the numbers of persons who had attended the club meetings and various outings. Of course, by the end of the war, those men still working on farms were usually directed in their occupation in the interest of the war effort. The production of food and clothing was a part of the war effort of the highest priority, not only for the maintenance of the services engaged in the Pacific, but to feed the population of the United Kingdom. Indeed the latter remained an urgent necessity for some years after the war ended. Needless to say, the Young Farmers' Club gave me a great deal of interest, some variety in my weekly duties, and indeed contact with a very pleasant number of young people. We were at Nelson about a year before the war ended, and as each of the courses lasted a few months, the personnel changed several times in that period.

August 1945 was the end of the war and word was passed round the station one morning that an announcement would be made over the public address system, and we were to stand outside our work places to hear the communication. It was President Truman announcing that the Japanese had surrendered on all fronts, followed by an official announcement from the CO that we were to carry on with our normal work pending further instructions.

Arrangements for demobilisation had been made some time before, and personnel were released on a 'points system' – marital status and possession of children were top qualifications, and also length of service overseas. As it was no longer necessary to supply technical staff for service in combat zones, personnel under training were released fairly rapidly in succeeding months. My colleagues, the education officers, were all senior to me, and also married with families, so by December I found myself the only education officer left on station. The technical officers, and some of the NCOs were permanent air force staff, as distinct from the rest of us who served for the duration of the war, and afterwards until no longer required. Naturally, the permanent staff were interested in their future prospects; the Chief of Air Staff did a tour of all stations, and addressed the officers at each station. He was able to give a general idea of the proposed peace-time establishment of the RNZAF and accordingly of the probable future employment of regular staff.

To sum up this account of my war service, it is obvious that I was fortunate and had derived a good deal of experience. My war service was unusual in that it included infantry and artillery units in the army, as well as air force experience, most of which was in fact teaching. In the course of frequent transfers from one unit to another, I had worked with a wide range of characters, ability and interests among the men who comprised the various units, and service in the ranks and in commissioned rank gave additional valuable experience. Very few indeed were individuals with whom I should not have wished to associate in civilian life.

But most importantly, it must be recorded that war conditions were directly responsible for introducing me to my future wife. As occurred with many servicemen, the changes in associations, resulting from the location of individuals in places and circumstances which would not have occurred in pre-war society, brought about marriages which would not otherwise have taken place. In all ways my marriage was most fortunate, as will appear later in this narrative, and this comment is written some years after my wife's unexpected death in December 1991.

We were married in Wellington, my wife's home city, on 12 December 1945. For the remainder of my service in the air force as a married officer I lived off station. Returning to Nelson after Christmas we stayed with friends till the station closed in January after which it became a civil airport. Posted to Wigram station, Christchurch, we lived in a flat in the city. For a few weeks, I took returned air crew for mathematics; they were a delightful group of young men, who had been selected as pilots for the commercial air service.

Three further postings followed: to Whenuapai, on Auckland Harbour; to Ardmore, south of the city; and finally to Hobsonville, which was the base for the flying-boat squadron. At Ardmore, I saw the first jet aircraft to arrive in New Zealand from England, to the great interest of all on the air station. From Ardmore, the RNZAF component of the British Commonwealth Occupation Force left for Japan, among whom was my younger brother Edmund, an instrument repairer. During this time, my wife and I had three lodgings in Auckland – a rented unit, and then with two friends successively. I was demobbed from the RNZAF on 26 May 1946.

Federation of Malaysia: Malaya and Singapore.

Chapter 4
Service in Malaya: the Colonial Service

Introduction to Malaya: Taiping, 1946–1948

In the concluding months of the war, the Colonial Office, London, circulated a brochure to all commands of all services in the Empire, inviting applications from servicemen and women for appointments in the Colonial Service. The circular, designated 'RDW6', included a message from the Secretary of State for the Colonies, Mr Oliver Stanley, briefly setting out the aims of the Service, which were to foster by every means the welfare of the peoples in the countries of the Colonial Empire, which numbered over fifty, large and small – some very small. As it is now over 30 years after the Empire ceased to exist, a brief explanation of the situation is necessary.

Julius Caesar commented that ancient Gaul was in three parts – so was the Colonial Empire, but with rather larger parts than those of Gaul. The Dominions – Canada, Australia, New Zealand and South Africa, with smaller units such as Newfoundland – were in communication with the Dominions Office; the Indian Empire, with adjoining Burma, was in contact with the India Office, and the Colonial Office supervised the remainder, the actual 'colonies'.

In the British Government, there were three distinct departments, each headed by a member of the Cabinet designated the 'Secretary of State'. The Secretary of State for the Colonies had wide powers; for those of us who were Colonial Servants, he was very much our 'boss': our appointments were officially his decisions; he arbitrated where necessary on our conditions of service and on any service problems which arise in a large organisation, and in particular regarding any question of the dismissal of an officer. Like the apostle St Paul, we could at the last resort 'appeal to Caesar'. As the Service had gradually evolved since the time of Charles II in the 1660s, it was the oldest public service of its kind in the western world; its principles were well known by all the officers in the Service, from the governor of each Territory to the most recent junior recruit, and

I personally know of no case which had to be referred to the Secretary of State in London.

It so happened that both the adjutant and his assistant on the Nelson RNZAF station were Malayan planters, who spoke glowingly of the country and its people. The Colonial Office had for years been recruiting officers from the Dominions – a statement to this effect was published in our university handbook in Auckland. For some reason unknown to me, New Zealanders recruited to the Colonial Service went to the African colonies – they were the largest and the most numerous part of the Service, and I suppose a tradition had been built up over the years. I do not know the reason for this preference, as I know no one who joined the Service from New Zealand. Apart from the recommendations of my two friends on the Nelson RNZAF station, Malaya was obviously closer to New Zealand, and from my study and reading I was more attracted to the East than to Africa. We were asked on our application form to specify the Territories preferred so I had no difficulty in this regard. In New Zealand, applications were to go to the Office of the Governor-General through the official channels, so I handed my form to the adjutant. Quite honestly, I was prepared to get nothing more than an acknowledgement.

However, in due course I received notice to appear for interview at Government House, Wellington. The Selection Board was chaired by the Governor-General, Sir Cyril Newall OM, head of the Air Staff, RAF, during and previous to the Battle of Britain (1937–1940), and included, among others, the Chief Justice and the Director of Education. When I arrived, the ante-room was full of service personnel; the senior officer was a commander in the navy, and the junior a sergeant in the RNZAF; from memory the largest number of candidates were about my rank – a flying officer in the air force equates with lieutenant in the army and sub-lieutenant in the navy. Of course, I never saw any of the applicants again, and have wondered how many were selected; it can be assumed that all of us who attended that morning had the recommendation of our immediate superiors, so it may well have been that all of us received appointments. The Service in Malaya in my time was never staffed up to the full establishment right to the date of independence.

As mentioned above, Yvonne and I were married two weeks before Christmas, and we had Christmas dinner on a cold day, with snow on the ranges which surround Wellington; in the New Year I returned to Nelson as the sole education officer on the station. By this time there were very few personnel on station, and we were concerned entirely with 'tidying up' and dealing with the remaining equipment. Material that was worn out or damaged was produced to a 'board' – from memory, two officers who decided the action to be taken – most of it was jettisoned to the rubbish dump.

About the end of January I was posted to Wigram, Christchurch, where I stayed for about three weeks, and then to Auckland, where I did about a month on each of three stations: Whenuapai, the main flying station in Auckland; Ardmore, south of Auckland where the RNZAF component of the British Commonwealth Occupation Force for Japan was assembled; and Hobsonville, the sea-plane station. Sea-planes did not last very long after the war, because land planes were more economic, and the station became the home of the peace-time TTS.

While all these postings were taking place, progressive advices were received of my Colonial Service application: notification that my application was recommended to the Colonial Office; then appointment to the Education Service, Malaya; and lastly instructions to contact the British High Commissioner in Wellington regarding a passage to Malaya.

As I had no priority 'points' from my war-time service to entitle me to demobilisation, I was informed that I would be released only when I had a date for embarkation for Malaya. In May this notice duly arrived, and I relinquished my commission on 26 May with 14 days' leave beforehand. This was just sufficient time to enable me to embark on the *Highland Princess*, a troopship formerly of the Royal Mail Line to South America, on 29 May, in a severe gale which is a common phenomenon in Wellington.

Advice previously received from the Colonial Office was that conditions in Malaya were not suitable for women to return to the country, but that men could travel on allocation of a passage, with the proviso that we should take sufficient camping gear to enable us to live outside government accommodation – i.e. stretcher, bed linen, cooking utensils, and so on, contained in a large army knapsack. Suitcases of clothes and several cases of books required in teaching made up the luggage. Three days before I was to sail, word was received that women were now permitted to travel to Malaya, but it was impossible for Yvonne to have the necessary inoculations or to obtain a passport and travel documents in the time remaining. A spare berth on a ship was, in itself, an unlikely event. Of course, Yvonne's inability to travel was a deep disappointment to us both. As my instructions in March were to the effect that the military administration would last for some months longer, we had not had the slightest indication that there was any possibility of Yvonne accompanying me.

The *Highland Princess* was still very much a troopship, and my sleeping quarters comprised tiers of bunks, about twelve to a cabin. The dining room was quite pleasant and had reverted more to peacetime conditions. The interesting thing, however, was that the signs were still in Spanish and Portuguese (the languages of Brazil), so we could imagine ourselves in the company of the wealthy travellers from Rio, Montevideo and Buenos Aires.

As everyone at that time was aware, the Japanese entry into the war was perhaps the greatest surprise in history. After the outbreak of the war in Europe, Europeans working in eastern countries spent their leave periods in Australia and New Zealand. It was obviously both difficult and dangerous to make the journey to Britain, and Malayan government officials were only permitted to go to Britain on extreme compassionate grounds. Thus, from 1940 onwards, there were a considerable number of government officials, planters and business people on leave in the Antipodes. Furthermore, many families had anticipated events, and many wives and children were sent to Australia and New Zealand for the duration of the war, while the men stayed on duty in Malaya. Thus it happened that on board the *Highland Princess* were many Malayans, planters, miners, government officials and some women who had been on leave in New Zealand when the Japanese invasion struck.

The voyage to Fremantle took about 12 days, with one day spent at Sydney. Arrangements had been made for me to meet Yvonne's great uncle, a retired bank manager, at the Australian Club in Macquarie Street. He entertained me with lunch and left me to read in the library, until I had to return to the ship. He did the same for Yvonne when she later called at Sydney. He died while we were on our first tour in Malaya.

We reached Fremantle on 10 June, which was Victory Day throughout the Commonwealth. I found that no arrangements had been made for my accommodation in Perth, where we were to stay a week awaiting our passage to Singapore on the Blue Funnel Line *Charon*. However, I accompanied two planters from the ship who had been booked in at a city hotel, and fortunately they had available a very pleasant room for me. A sidelight on the times: on going to bed, I found that the door to my room not only would not lock, but simply had no lock. On enquiring at the reception desk, I was told, 'Oh, don't worry, we don't bother with locking doors here.' Years afterwards, when living in Perth, a journalist reported on a trip to the United States, when he met Bob Hope, a prominent film personality and also well known as an entertainer to the troops in the Pacific. When the Perth journalist introduced himself, Bob Hope said, 'Oh, you're from Perth, where they don't have locks on hotel doors.' Sadly, things changed greatly while we lived in Perth in later years.

We were instructed to board the *Charon* on the Sunday night, and the ship departed early next morning. The passengers included those who had come from New Zealand, with a number of women from Western Australia, wives of men who had lived in Malaya pre-war, returning to meet up with their menfolk who had gone on ahead. I found the journey, both from Wellington and then from Fremantle to Singapore, a most useful introduction to the country. The conversation at mealtimes and elsewhere was about life in Malaya, in all its aspects. Of course, the Malaya described was that of before the Japanese invasion, but it did give me a good description of what life in the country was like.

Not everyone on the ship was going to Malaya or Singapore. One man was the Hong Kong Shanghai bank manager in Sourabaya, Java. I have often wondered how he fared, as the Dutch never regained their control over the East Indies, now entitled Indonesia. Others at my table included the wife of a judge in Burma, another country which has not fared well since the war. The only other New Zealander whom I recollect was a lawyer taking up a position in Malaya as district judge; for much of the war he had been a liaison officer with the army in Russia.

The *Charon* and its sister ship *Gorgon* were of the Blue Funnel Line (Liverpool) and had been on the Fremantle–Singapore run some years before the war. A third ship, *Centaur*, was lost by enemy action. These vessels had accommodation for sixty passengers, and the lower decks were adapted to carry sheep 'on the hoof' from the north-west Australian ports to Singapore, and on the return journey, cattle from these ports to Fremantle. The cargo included food products for the Singapore market – cases of oranges and apples were carried in the open on the decks. The ships thus performed a most useful service to Western Australia and Singapore; from the point of view of Europeans in Singapore and Malaya, Western Australia was the nearest source of temperate fruits and European food.

A common holiday tour for Western Australians was the round trip to Singapore and back, and there were always on the ship passengers doing this tour. The presence of the animals below decks was normally not noticeable, and only objectionable on the upper decks in hot weather when there was no wind. The ships had British officers, and crews (mostly Chinese) recruited from Singapore. The latter were polite and efficient, and could be communicated with in 'bazaar Malay', the patois used in Malaya by all races in daily dealings in the markets and shops. In Perth I saw some Malay grammars, which I bought and studied during the voyage to Singapore. I was not able to communicate well with the crew on my first voyage, but this was no problem on the later trips.

There were only two real shocks for me in my service in Malaya, each of which occurred on my arrival in Singapore and Taiping. The *Charon* reached Singapore about midday on a Thursday, the voyage having taken 11 days, including a day each at the ports of Onslow and Derby. My two weeks in Suva (18° S) in the army, which anyhow was in the autumn, did not prepare me for stepping into a steam bath, which impressed me as the climate of Singapore, which is near the equator. My first reaction was, 'How on earth am I going to live in this climate, let alone perform any useful work?' After berthing at Singapore, the ship was boarded by transport agents, all of them in my recollection from Chinese firms, except one, who was an Australian of many years' residence, who appeared even at that hour rather to be 'under the influence'. We passengers looked at each other: I sensed that the Australian was what he said he was, and he had about six coolies with him, Chinese and Indians who seemed to hang on his every word. Quite clearly he had their confidence.

There were two returning planters among the passengers, and together we decided to put our trust in the Australian. His paperwork was well up to scratch, and there was provision for insurance. From newspapers on the ship, and comments by passengers and the officers, we had gathered that the situation in Singapore and Malaya was very bad as regards law and order, of which more will be said later. As we all wanted our personal effects to meet us at our destinations, the outcome of our decision was of the highest importance. And it may be remembered that my advice from the Colonial Office was that I might for some time have to camp in a school, and possibly cook my own meals. Further, I had several fruit cases full of books required for teaching, and I had anticipated, correctly as it turned out, that I should have to rely on these for some time to do my work. I may mention that all of my effects, except one case of books, reached me in Taiping. Most of my companions were not so fortunate.

An officer from the Malayan Establishment Office, which was in charge of our postings and service conditions generally, met us on the ship and directed us to the office in Singapore. Again I was fortunate in being in the company of 'old hands' who knew how to get to the address given. I recall that we travelled there in the ubiquitous Singapore taxis, which appeared to consist of Morris Minors and similar cars. At the office, a very pleasant official gave me my posting to King Edward VII School, Taiping, in North Perak. The official said that he knew Taiping, which was a very pleasant town, and the school was an old and highly regarded institution. My companions guided me to a hotel, where we had dinner, prior to boarding the night passenger train to Kuala Lumpur. When we got to the train, about dusk at 6 p.m., I was considerably cheered to note that the climate was pleasantly cool.

The journey of about 250 miles to Kuala Lumpur took all night, about twelve hours in all. Singapore Island is quite small and only 17 miles took us to the causeway across the Straits of Johore, barely a mile wide at this point. There were still some rubber estates on the island, as well as cultivated areas growing products for the food markets. As the train stopped for long periods at the larger towns, perhaps up to an hour, I was able for the first time to experience the sights, sounds and smells of the East, together with the continual kaleidoscope afforded by the polyglot population of Malaya. Johore Bahru, the State capital of Johore, and very much its largest town, with a population then of about 50,000, was our first stop; it was also the customs station at the point of entry to Malaya, which was a separate country from the Colony of Singapore. I do not remember that we were questioned; I suppose that it could be assumed that train travellers had with them mainly their personal effects.

But the scene on the station platform was what concerned me. I was completely fascinated with its infinite variety, comprising a mixture of races, a crowd of all ages and both sexes, the range of clothing and costume, and the equally diverse range of occupations. As is inevitable in the East, any occasion or situation which may give opportunity for trading in any form, attracts a crowd of buyers and sellers. The wayside food stall, consisting of a cooking medium and a variety of food, is an invariable part of the scene. Just as common are vendors of fruits and vegetables; as they were in season, I was introduced to the pungent smell of the durian, a large fruit about the size of a melon; the smell and taste are too strong for European taste, but most Asians regard it as a delicacy. Malaya has a wide selection of fruits, including many varieties of banana, from the very large to the quite small, in size about that of a thumb; the latter is the 'golden banana' (pisang mas) much prized for its sweet and distinctive flavour. Similar animated, noisy crowds were present at each station until we reached Kuala Lumpur, the numbers of people at each station being less as we advanced through the night.

At Kuala Lumpur, we were given seats in a day carriage in the train to Penang, which left about an hour after we arrived from Singapore. Here it must be mentioned that Penang is an island, but the train tickets covered the ferry trip, of about three miles, from the railway terminus at the port, Butterworth, to the island.[6] The distance to Taiping from Kuala Lumpur was over 200 miles, and took till about six o'clock in the evening. My companions on this journey were a Plymouth Brethren missionary, a New Zealander, and her two charges, Chinese girls, whom she was escorting to their home in Taiping. The missionary had served in Taiping before the war, and was returning to continue her work with the mission. During the day, we saw common features of the landscape – jungle, rubber plantations, rice fields and tin mining dredges. My companion was able to talk about the industries and the life of the people, which made the day pass very pleasantly until we reached Taiping.

I hired a taxi which took me to the school, where I was directed to the principal's house, next door. There I found the principal and my colleague, the other 'European master', a Welshman, J.D.R. Howell, who both made me feel welcome, conducted me to the government Rest House opposite for dinner, and informed me that I was to stay in the principal's house until my wife arrived. The principal, F.C. Barraclough, was again to be my official superior when I went to Klang, Selangor. The principal's wife had not accompanied her husband to Malaya on that tour. As stated earlier, I was on the first ship to bring women from Australia to Malaya, and few officers had set up their homes, pending their wives' arrival. Thus most European officers dined at the Rest House, which was a sort of European club.

The next day was a Saturday, and I was told that there were classes and other activities, one being a debate which was held each week for the senior classes. I was to teach English and history, and as I had the status of senior English master, the debates were part of my portfolio. As most of the English schools in Malaya admitted children from the age of 6 and saw them through their school career to the top class, the School Certificate, boys' schools included women staff who taught the lowest classes, termed 'primary' classes. I found that the entire staff had turned out to welcome me. In a fortunate life I have had many kindly welcomes, but none in which I felt so completely at ease and 'at home'. There was no feeling, however slight, of being a stranger to them from a strange country – the only other New Zealander in the Education Department was the deputy director,[7] soon afterwards to become the director of education. Though, as will be seen, quite difficult problems appeared during our stay in the country, this feeling of really 'belonging' never changed until the day came for us to end our service and say farewell.

Then came the second shock, which I mentioned earlier. The debate was held in the school hall, and followed a common arrangement. There were three speakers for and against the motion, opportunity for contributions from the floor and summing up by the leaders. The chairman was the school captain. As the boys spoke, I scarcely understood a word! At this time (June 1946) the boys had been back at school a little over six months, after nearly four years of Japanese occupation, during which the use of English was forbidden, with savage penalties for any attempts to contravene the ban. So I asked myself, 'How am I to understand these boys, or they me?' However, as with the climate, I soon got used to the conditions, and found that my ears adapted to the dialect (for such it was and still is). Each race in Malaya speaks English with a different accent and intonation, but overall there is a pleasant lilt in the speech, and after many years in Australia I still believe I can pick out those Chinese and Indians who come from Malaysia – and there are many of them, mostly very useful additions to the population of Australia.

The next few months were extremely busy, as many strategies were put in train in order to be able to function in the new environment.[8] School lessons took more time to prepare than usual, as I had not taught the subjects for over four years during the break of war service, and in addition there was a considerable difference in the syllabuses and therefore in the subject matter. As already mentioned, getting attuned to the ways of Asian students added another dimension to the practice of teaching, but did not prove, fortunately, as difficult as appeared at first sight. School hours were 7.45 a.m. to 1.15 p.m., so as to avoid the very hot period of the day. We resumed at about 5 p.m. for sports and other extra-classroom activities, such as drama, debating and scouting.

New recruits to the Colonial Service had to serve three years before confirmation in appointment, the main factor in which was a pass in the government language examinations. Of the three main languages spoken in the country, the vast majority of European officers took Malay. Chinese (Mandarin) was taken by a minority of administrative officers and police and a few others, of whom one was an education officer. The Labour Department was mainly concerned with the labour force on estates, mainly Tamils, so officials dealing with this community learnt Tamil; again one education officer who supervised the Tamil schools was Tamil speaking. Everyone else had to pass in Malay, in which there were three grades.

The elementary stage, 'Standard I', was taken by the majority, such as engineers, who were required to use the language in speaking to labourers, people in villages and shops about minor daily matters.

Three departments – the Administrative, whose officers made up the 'Malayan Civil Service', Education and Customs – had to pass 'Standard II', which would be at least equivalent to second-year degree level and included translation from and into the language, knowledge of set books in Malay classics, history and Malay life and customs. A conversation test formed part of each examination. The highest grade, 'Standard III', carried a bonus if passed within two years from entry, was optional, and about equivalent to an honours subject in an Arts degree. Obviously, passing the language examination was top priority and arrangements were made for each officer on arrival to employ a native teacher or 'Munshi', who was paid by the government at a stated rate per hour. I was again extremely fortunate in having the senior Malay master in the school, whose English was of course excellent, and he could explain points of grammar. This was important, as a European education officer could be called upon to teach in Malay; as will be seen later, this occurred in my experience. More commonly, we were engaged sometimes in inspecting Malay schools, so a good grasp of the language was necessary if this duty was to be effective. I completed the Standard II examination within two years – examinations were arranged every six months – and this was an average time taken by the European officers.

The main aftermath of the Japanese occupation, in a physical sense, was the deterioration in buildings, roads and railways, and of course in mechanical equipment. The destruction of the bridges was almost the only sign of actual damage, and this had been mainly carried out by the British in their retreat to Singapore. The Public Works Department (PWD) carried out restoration work as required. As noted earlier, the school and the principal's house had been in use for some time before my arrival. Returning married officers were requested to keep in touch with the PWD engineer as to the date when wives and families were expected to return, and official quarters were assigned accordingly. After I arrived in Taiping, my wife informed me that we could expect our first child early in the New Year. It was October, four months after my arrival, that a passage was first available for Yvonne, and as there were so few ships on the route from New Zealand to Fremantle, she was flown to Perth, a rare privilege at the time, as air services were even less available than sea transport. I travelled down to Singapore to meet Yvonne, and we made the journey to Taiping by train. As our own quarters were not ready, the principal kindly invited us to stay in his house until we could move into our own residence.

A break in the regular round of school duties and Malay language study included a trip up and down the Malayan railway system which I undertook during the August school holidays. The school year approximated that of Australia and New Zealand with the annual examinations in November or December, instead of in May or June as in Britain. The holidays at the end of the year were four weeks, mid-December to January; in addition there were two weeks about April, and four weeks in August, which coincided with part of the northern school vacation. Accordingly, I took a week's 'local leave' (we were allowed two weeks annually), travelled down to Singapore, returned to Kuala Lumpur, and then went north to Penang, finally completing the short distance back to Taiping. I spent a day in each of the three centres, much the largest in the country. This was sufficient for me to find my way about, know where to hail taxis, and sample the facilities of leading hotels, including 'Raffles' in Singapore, and the 'E and O' in Penang. (Each of these were old hotels and much used by Europeans.) The brief acquaintanceship was helpful in saving time when I went to a city on duty or on holiday, and of course the journey passed through the most important areas in the country for population or industry, notably rubber plantations and tin mining operations.

When I returned I found that there had been a change of principal, a Welshman replacing a Yorkshireman, who had been sent to the UK on long leave. The 'long leave' for European officers was calculated on an increasing scale, six months' leave after four years' service for junior officers under 35 years of age, then six months after three years for older persons, the tours of duty reducing with age. During the later years of service a 'tour' might be two years or less, but followed by a shorter spell on leave. Of course, when civil government resumed in April 1946, everyone had just had some leave, the majority after spending the three and a half years as prisoners in Changi Gaol, Singapore. To get the system going again, senior officers were sent on leave after a few months' duty, not an undesirable procedure, as many had not made a complete recovery when they had returned to duty. It was a point of personal honour for the pre-war officers to return at the earliest possible moment, and this was sometimes done with the unwilling concurrence of the Colonial Office medical officers.

The new principal, J.D. Joseph, was a younger man, but also an ex-Changi prisoner; he had been a keen rugby footballer in his younger days, and still was one of the leading referees in the country. The immediate scholastic problem was to get the pupils through their School Certificate Examination, after the four-year gap during the 'Japanese time'. So a meeting of upper school staff was held to discuss what extra classes were needed to give the boys the best chance of passing in the December examinations. The main concern was expressed in such subjects as mathematics and geography, where the background normally built up in the previous years was 'very rusty' or completely lacking. Each teacher was asked to give his assessment of progress in his subjects. I asked to keep the share of the timetable which I already had, but considered that no further time was needed. The extra lessons took place in the afternoons or on Saturday mornings.

The staffing of the English schools needs explanation. Colonial Service staff supplied the principals of the larger schools and one to three assistants, depending on the size of the school. The rest of the staff comprised Raffles College graduates in the secondary school, and 'normal trained' staff in the primary school and lower secondary classes. The latter were trained on the old 'pupil teacher' system. Qualifying in the School Certificate Examination with at least a credit in English language, pupils spent three years as pupil teachers taking classes on Saturday mornings in English language and written composition, English literature, and principles and practice of teaching. Each year they sat a written examination and had a class inspection by a departmental officer. I was asked to take two classes in English language and literature as from August 1946, when the schools reopened after the vacation. So from this date onwards the English school system had reverted to the pre-war organisation – still less than twelve months after the end of the Japanese occupation. I think all of us who participated in these classes enjoyed our association with the young people in training, whose general attitude was excellent.

The period of Japanese occupation in Malaya may be considered simply as an evil inflicted on an innocent civilian occupation. More important than the brutal forays of the Kempeitai, or secret police, was the fact that the country was in a state of chaos, and food was in desperately short supply. Malaya had never been self-supporting in rice production, and over half the amount needed for consumption in the pre-war period was imported from the northern neighbours, Thailand, Burma and Indo-China, and paid for by exports generated by the major industries. Thus, during the war, the main occupation of the entire population was the basic necessity of ensuring mere survival, and most people, parents in particular, would spend the entire day searching for food to keep the children alive.

Returning to the English schools, pupils were admitted at the age of 6 years, on the 1st of January, and not over 8 years at that date.

Pupils were allowed to fail any class once in their school career; a second failure meant that their age was above that allowed for the class, and they were required to leave. Of course, starting at 6 years gave an extra year available to complete the school course, and most children were admitted at this age.

Thus, when the schools reopened in 1945 after the Japanese surrender in September, all pupils who would have attended in 1942 were admitted, up to four years older than the normal age for their classes, and the lowest class had children aged 6 years to 10 years. Similarly, the School Certificate class, whose normal age would be 17 years, had young men and women of 21 years, most of whom would have been working to help their families survive. From recollection, only pupils who had married were refused admission, which in an Asian country meant that there were fewer girls than boys in the upper classes. Naturally, the schools were encouraged to return to normal conditions as quickly as possible, and in the primary classes especially, pupils were promoted to a higher class as soon as teachers considered they were able to cope with the work of that class. The primary schools were thus swamped with these post-war entrants for several years, as in effect they were coping with those eligible to enter school in the period of ten years, instead of the normal six-year course.

There was another phenomenon which had its effect on the flood of enrolments in all schools after the war – an actual revolution in the attitude of the people towards education – a general attitude among all races and all classes that education was the means of personal and national advancement.[9] Pre-war education was in general middle class and, more specifically, male. There were some differences in attitude between the three races, but two general trends were common to all.

First, formal education for girls has never been a tradition for any of the races. Immediately pre-war, in Malay schools only about one in four of the pupils was a girl; in the Chinese schools, the girls on admission numbered about half the total of the boys, and did not attend school for as many years; the Indian schools did a little better than the Chinese. Even in the English schools, the preserve of the middle class, Chinese and Indian girls numbered only half the boys' total, Malay girls only one tenth the number of boys. Only the Eurasians sent their sons and daughters to school in equal numbers. As will be shown later, this small community had an influence on Malayan life far in excess of their proportion of the total population.

By 1941, the outbreak of the Japanese war, the British had ruled Singapore, Penang and Malacca for over 120 years, and been influential in the Malay States, Perak and Selangor, for nearly 70 years; the educational achievement had been reached by devoted work and persuasion by many gifted and devoted teachers, including those in Christian missions, but progress had clearly been very slow. In Taiping, Yvonne and I met some of the original missionaries, who had founded the girls' schools. The school principals told us of knocking on the doors of wealthy merchants and doctors, begging them to let their girls go for English education. The girls were taken to and from schools in rickshaws, or accompanied by servants.

Second, education for Malay girls in Malay schools was unknown before 1920, and only in the 1930s was opposition lessening enough for parents to consider sending their daughters to train as teachers. In all ways, especially in education, the war was a tragedy, disregarding entirely the physical impact of the war itself. Change was in the air, and the country would have been immeasurably more advanced, with the benefit of gradual and planned development, if the war had not happened. In spite of the chaos following the Japanese surrender, when the British military administration ended in March 1946, the enrolments in most types of schools had reached the 1941 level, and the English schools had actually increased their enrolment by nearly one third. During our time in Malaya, the greatest demand made upon the Education Department was to meet the demand for places in every type of school. This in turn meant that the provision of sites for schools, buildings, teachers and their training facilities never caught up with the volume of enrolments, right to the date of independence in 1957.

The arrival of Yvonne heralded a fresh round of activity in setting up our home, actually our first, as we had only had a succession of boarding arrangements while I was in the RNZAF. Soon after arrival, the PWD engineer took Yvonne to see some government houses which could be made available for us. The houses were all in their unkempt occupation condition, but Yvonne chose a house about 200 yards from the school – two storeys, bedrooms upstairs, lounge, dining room and study downstairs. We were told afterwards that the house had been seen by other possible tenants, but rejected on account of its grimy appearance, despite an assurance that the building would be cleaned and painted.

We were very pleased with our choice. The house was ready for occupation in about two weeks, until which time we were guests of the principal, J.D. Joseph. In his early years in Malaya, he had served in the King Edward VII School as a master, and consequently knew many people in the town, especially the 'old boys' of 20 years previously, with whom he was very popular. He took infinite trouble to assist every boy in his charge, was an inspiring principal and a charming host. We owed a great deal to him for his friendship and guidance in our early months in the country. His wife was on a ship evacuating women from Singapore when war broke out; the ship was subsequently sunk by the Japanese.

On his return from leave, J.D. Joseph arrived with a charming Welsh lady as his second wife. Shortly afterwards he was transferred to Singapore as principal of the first teachers' college for English school teachers. Previously, as described elsewhere, these teachers had been trained as 'normal class' students, required to attend at lectures concurrently with full-time teaching. It was many years afterwards that the first English school teachers' college was established in Malaya. Sadly, Joseph was badly injured in an assault in a riot in Singapore which erupted while he was driving home in the city one evening. He returned to duty, but never completely recovered, and died shortly afterwards while on sick leave in Wales. His death removed an able teacher whose contribution in the years leading to independence would have been invaluable.

Close and friendly relationships existed between the government and 'aided' schools, that is, those run by the church missions. As commonly in Malayan towns, of the two girls' English schools in Taiping, one was Catholic of the Order of the Holy Infant Jesus, the other methodist, of the American Episcopal Methodist Mission. The Catholic convents included an orphanage for destitute or deserted children, whom they brought up and educated, and the girls were highly sought after as wives. We were advised to contact the mother superior about a servant and she sent us a Tamil, Mary, whose husband had been a clerk on a rubber estate pre-war, and who had been killed by the Japanese. From then on Mary had found refuge in the convent and we of course were most fortunate to employ her. She had one son, and stayed with us until she died, shortly before we left Kuala Lumpur, on our final departure from the country.

By the time Christmas arrived, we had settled into our new home, had got to know the school staff and their families, and could find our way round the streets and to the shops that supplied Europeans. In each town there was a shop, usually Chinese, that supplied refrigerated foods – meat, fruit and temperate climate vegetables. The large supplier of refrigerated goods was the Singapore Cold Storage Company, which was in fact Australian owned. It was said that their large establishment in Singapore could supply any kind of food produced anywhere in the world. The British preponderated among the population, which included people from all countries in Western Europe and from North America, all of whom had their individual preference for foods 'from home'. The result of this wide provenance of food, and let it be said also of drink, was to make available an infinite variety of diet for all races. Each community in general followed the customs and culture of its national origins, but probably every middle-class family had recourse to some products of other races, though normally it kept to a traditional style.

The import of overseas foods served to increase the range of variety already present in the country, as the Chinese and Indians originated from a wide range of provinces in their homelands, and there were quite different customs, regarding both food and dress, from one Malay state to another. This vast range of customs, language, dress and religion constituted a main attraction of the country for most of us who spent some years working in Malaya.

As may be imagined, among the many problems facing the government after the Japanese occupation was a complete breakdown of law and order. I have mentioned that I was lucky to receive delivery of my personal effects, except for one case of books. Numerous stories were told, almost daily, of the troubles encountered regarding, especially, thefts. It was said that personal luggage disappeared during the night while passengers slept on the trains; one man tied his suitcases to his leg before he went to sleep and was awakened sometime later by a thief trying to cut the cords before removing the property. Serviceable motor vehicle tyres were especially valuable. The district judge was a young Englishman, an ex-RAF pilot. He had his car parked on the street outside his bedroom window, and in the early hours saw some thieves jacking up the car, preparatory to removing the tyres. He raised the alarm, the thieves were caught and received the maximum sentence next day. The story was that after this, anyone up before the judge could expect the maximum sentence for this crime. (Incidentally, the judge's wife was French and when they came to dinner with us Yvonne could converse well – she had been to a convent of a French order – so the evening was a success.)

One of the customs officers went home on leave, and was married; apparently the families were well connected and they received many wedding presents to start their married life in Malaya. The presents duly reached Singapore and were put in a 'sealed railway wagon' for transport to Taiping. The only thing to arrive at Taiping was the wagon, its sealed doors wrenched open, and not one article left in it. As a result an SOS went round the European community and we combined to give them sufficient articles to set up home. As luck would have it, Yvonne brought with her many household articles, which with my 'camping equipment' referred to above, enabled us to make a useful contribution.

The several years after the war were marked inevitably by a post-war austerity, as the industries of European countries required several years to rebuild. Some items were strictly controlled by government regulation, one being motor vehicles, which meant that official approval was necessary before a car could be purchased. Permits were granted only to those whose work required the use of a car – police, officials in various departments who had inspecting duties, or those who lived some distance from public transport, such as miners or rubber planters.

In the Education Department, officials concerned with inspecting schools were able to purchase a car; those of us who were occupied in school duties were not. But such was the general attitude of friendly cooperation that essential trips to doctors or hospitals were met by car owners, cars being lent with drivers. Government officers, and most planters and mining managers, employed a driver. Apart from the convenience, it could on occasion be essential that the car was available to move off at a moment's notice, as will appear later in this account.

Taiping was the original capital of Perak when the British first took charge in the 1870s. The former garrison church, All Saints, had plaques on the walls in remembrance of the regiments who had served there, as well as of prominent officials and parishioners. My memory is that the Japanese did not vandalise or damage the churches, and this applied to St Andrew's Cathedral, Singapore.

Taiping accordingly was the location of the largest prison in Malaya. The houses of government officials included those of the British Resident, the senior official in the State, and the heads of government departments. As the capital was moved after the war to Ipoh, about 50 miles south and much the largest city in the State, the residences constituted surplus accommodation. When I arrived, Taiping was the headquarters of the 6th Indian Division, and the Residency was occupied by the general officer commanding and the other residences by his senior staff. Round the town one saw the Regimental Headquarters, and mornings and evenings were filled with the sound of bugles announcing reveille and last post. The only one I now recall is the Jat Regiment, one of the most distinguished.[10]

For people from a temperate climate, such as Britain, the opportunity to retreat to a cooler atmosphere acted as a tonic in the official round of a tour of duty. Befitting the first British government centre in Malaya, Taiping had a 'hill station', Maxwell's Hill, something over 2,000 feet in altitude literally overlooking the town. Taiping is situated on a narrow coastal plain, only a few miles wide. The hills, running approximately north and south parallel to the coast, caused unusual vagaries in the climate, even by tropical standards. The average annual rainfall over the Malay Peninsula is about 90 inches, some areas as low as 60 inches, and others correspondingly more. However, Taiping had an average of about 200 inches, by far the heaviest of any populated area in the country.

As noted earlier, schools functioned from about 7.45 a.m. to 1.15 p.m. and then there was a 'siesta' until after 5 p.m. In Taiping, almost every day, there was a thunderstorm at about 4 p.m., with the usual tropical downpour lasting about an hour on average. After the rain, the atmosphere was pleasantly cool and fresh, and one felt like engaging in a game of tennis (the roads and the courts soon dried), cricket, football, or whatever game was on offer. There were a number of rugby teams supported by the military units. King Edward School had a rugby reputation, so in the wet season, August to December, there were rugby games most afternoons. As the principal, J.D. Joseph, was a rugby enthusiast, a New Zealander from a rugby country had no option but to fill a place in one of the adult teams, usually the 'Old Boys' against the School First XV. On one occasion, we played before the governor, Sir Edward Gent, who remarked to Joseph that some of the staff 'did not seem too fit'. Of course, on this day, the usual climate in Taiping failed to function. There was no afternoon rain, which meant that at 5 p.m. when we took the field it was a humid tropical afternoon at its worst, in full sunshine. Unfortunately, Sir Edward had a tragic end; returning to London for consultations after the Communist insurrection broke out, his plane crashed on landing, following a collision with another aircraft. Sir Edward was reported to be the principal originator of the ill-fated Malayan Union Constitution.

Yvonne and I managed to have three holidays on Maxwell's Hill in the successive Christmases from 1946 to 1948. The first occasion was made possible by another post-war achievement. A retired planter had been appointed manager of the hill station and had made Herculean efforts to get some of the bungalows ready for occupation, and we were among the first post-war visitors. At the altitude of over 2,000 feet, the evenings were cold enough to make a fire very welcome; the days were sunny and pleasantly warm. Access to the station was by a path, up which provisions were carried by coolies. Yvonne went up and down carried on a palanquin, while I walked the distance of about two miles. On our last visit a road had been constructed, passable by jeeps. Thus the hill station had passed in effect from the nineteenth to the twentieth century in two years.

Similar developments were to be commonplace during our time in the country.

When the anticipated time of arrival of our first child drew near, the district officer made available his car to convey Yvonne and me to the maternity hospital at Batu Gajah, a mining town about 10 miles south of Ipoh and about 80 miles south of Taiping. Kate was born the next week, February 1947, and the following week mother and daughter came home. On the three occasions we had the use of the district officer's car.

When the school reopened in January, the teachers had to get acquainted with new classes and to make the usual arrangements to initiate the year's programme, for both the teaching and the external activities. The main interest in the first term was the results of the School Certificate Examination held in the previous December. The overall school result was very good indeed – there was only one failure among the total of sixty boys who had sat the examination.

Each paper was assessed in four grades – 'A' distinction, 'C' credit, 'P' pass and 'F' fail; the main aim on the part of each teacher was, of course, to get as many 'A's in his subject as possible. In my subjects, there were many 'A's in English literature, not so many in English language (essay, comprehension, etc.) but none in history, though there was only one failure – the boy who failed the entire examination. The weekend after the arrival of the results, teams from the Taiping school went down to Ipoh for games with the government boys' school (Anderson School) which gave an opportunity for the teachers to 'compare notes' on the School Certificate results. I did not make the trip, I should think on account of the homecoming of my new daughter. However, my colleagues told me that Anderson School teachers were not so impressed with the results in mathematics, literature, etc. but enquired, 'But how did you go in history?' When the Taiping results were stated to contain almost all passes, the Ipoh teachers gasped, 'Most of ours failed' – it was the black spot in the total result. From memory, candidates usually took only one subject over the minimum required to gain a certificate, so a weakness in any one subject eliminated this safety margin. The following year the history results were again very good, and this time there were some 'A's; the 1947 students had been back at school two years, which gave them an advantage over those of the previous year. Though no doubt a small thing in itself, the history results contributed a fillip for the new recruit to the Service from New Zealand.[11]

As it was to prove later, the year 1947 was the only 'normal' year of our service in Malaya. My work at school was similar to what I had done the previous year, with the important advantage that I had had the experience of that year, and to some extent at least 'knew the ropes'. There was only one variation from my programme – teaching Latin. The School Certificate was in all respects similar to that taken in schools in England, and was an entrance qualification accepted by British universities. The wealthier families in Malaya had a tradition of sending gifted children to the UK for university education, and at this time Latin was an essential for admission to some universities, such as Oxford, Cambridge and London. Latin was taken as a special class in English schools for this purpose. Usually there was a member of a religious order in a Catholic school who provided this tuition, but in 1947 the brother (of the Order of Christian Brothers) had gone on leave. I had taken Latin to honours for my degree, and I volunteered to fill the gap. Pupils from the four schools, the two girls' schools already mentioned, the Catholic boys' school and King Edward VII formed the class of about a dozen or so. The School Certificate was a four year course, so for most of the class it was a question of completing the requirements in one year. We met an hour before the regular school assembly time of 8 a.m., for several days a week. The course consisted of the study of passages from the Latin texts, plus translation from and into Latin. An indication of the calibre of the students is given by the examination result – they all passed, several gaining 'A' and 'C' passes.

Two developments occurred at the end of the year. First, it became evident that we were to expect our second child in a few months, and simultaneously I was advised that I was to go to Selangor to assume duties as headmaster of the High School at Klang, the port city for Kuala Lumpur. It was agreed that the transfer would take place after the new member of the family arrived. However, our second daughter was in no hurry to make her appearance, so I left Taiping by train, accompanied by Kate in my cabin, in the lower bunk, and by our amah Mary, who travelled second class. Kate was just a year old and had been running (she rarely walked) since she was nine and a half months. The train left at 10 p.m. and we were invited to dinner by the engineer and his wife, who were duly entertained by Kate's activity.

Second post, Klang, 1948–1950 and leave in New Zealand, 1950–1951

We arrived in Kuala Lumpur next morning at about 7 a.m. and took the train to Klang on the branch line, a distance of about 24 miles, which took about an hour. Kate had slept all night and given no trouble, but she cried all the way to Klang, and nothing that amah or I did would pacify her. My predecessor met us at the station, and we moved straight into the headmaster's house. He had contacted the reverend mother of the Klang convent, who had arranged for us to have a second amah, a charming young Tamil woman, Annie, who also was to stay with us most of our time in the country. Annie was employed as children's amah, and her first problem was to chase Kate around the house trying to get her to eat her meals. A few days later, a telephone call came from Yvonne at Batu Gajah announcing Ruth's arrival, and Kate and I met them two weeks later at Kuala Lumpur.

Klang High School 1949; TKT headmaster with senior assistant and prefects

So we began our time in Klang in February 1948, when I had been in the Malayan Service for nineteen months. On a personal note, this made me the first student of my 1935 graduate group at Auckland Teachers' College to receive an appointment as principal.

Klang High School had been established about 1930 and the buildings, which included a Malay boys' hostel, headmaster's house and several teachers' quarters, had been built not long before the war. It was in all respects similar to King Edward VII School, Taiping, except it was smaller and had an enrolment of a thousand boys in my time. The school had had three headmasters in a little over two years since the war, two of whom were transferred because of health problems. The school games were soccer, hockey and cricket – rugby was not as widely played as it was in Perak. In class teaching, I took history and English with some of the upper classes. The senior local staff had been with the school pre-war, which of course was an asset in enabling a sound post-war development to take place.

My predecessor had asked that his Malay driver and his family continue to occupy the driver's quarters at the back of the garage adjoining the headmaster's house. As mentioned earlier, I had not yet acquired a car so this was no difficulty. In my first week at the school, I was working in the headmaster's office, when a really violent thunderstorm struck, with torrential rain. During the storm my amah Mary's son, Patrick, ran over to me saying that the driver's child was drowned in the drain near the garage. In fact, the storm had blown down a casuarina pine, severing the electric cable from the house to the garage, and the child, playing in the flooded drain, had touched the broken cable, still live, and been electrocuted. I pulled the child clear of the drain, and boys from the Malay hostel tried to revive her, but to no avail. The driver's wife had gone over to the hostel to talk to the matron before the storm and had left the family unattended. Of course, if the weather had stayed fine there would have been no danger and no tragedy.

Earlier in this account I stated that on the return of British rule the prime aim was to get the country functioning again, not necessarily meeting pre-war standards of efficiency, but at least functioning. As a result of the tragedy of the child's death, the Electricity Board engineer made an inspection of the wiring of the house, and reported that it was all in an advanced state of disintegration. We had been awakened a few times during the night by a flash in the ceiling, and in the morning there was the carcase of a dead rat to signify the cause of the flash. The child's death was clearly due to the same cause – the rubber insulation of the cable she grasped had perished. Needless to say, the house and garage were immediately rewired.

The only training colleges for teachers in pre-war Malaya were for Malay school teachers, for men at Tanjong Malim, on the border between Perak and Selangor, and at Malacca for women. As described above, local teachers for the English schools were trained as student teachers during three years, when they taught as class teachers during the week and attended 'normal classes' on Saturday mornings, in three subjects, English language, English literature and theory and practice of teaching. In practice, instructing in these normal classes constituted an extra duty for expatriate education officers, with whom, post-war, were included some senior local teachers.

In Taiping, as mentioned above, I was asked to teach the English language and literature classes soon after I arrived. When I arrived in Klang, I was asked to take over the instruction in theory and practice of teaching, which I continued during my time in Klang. For transport, I relied on the public bus service between Klang and Kuala Lumpur. None of my students was younger than 25 years of age, as that was the age of those who had passed their School Certificate in 1941. By some miracle, the examination papers completed in December 1941 had reached Cambridge, and the results were brought back to the country with the British troops who took over the country after the Japanese surrender. This remarkable stroke of luck made an excellent impression, not only on the students concerned. Actually many of the 'normal' students were much older, some several years older than I was. These all did well, as they had the benefit of maturity, among other advantages, and in a few years most of them were promoted to be heads of schools. As noted later, this acquaintance with numbers of younger teachers proved of great assistance to me in later years.

With our two children added for good measure, we found our time in Klang very full, and time passed interestingly and happily. With the support and to some extent the relief of the staff, in my first year I took one period of English with each class in the upper half of the school, mainly in speech training and reading and comprehension. There was a tendency by Asian staff to wait and see what a new head wanted. The school traditionally ran a concert in the first term (January to April) and when informed of this I did my best to infuse interest and enterprise into the preparations for the event. Of course, the success of the concert depended mainly on how well the boys aged 6 years to about 20 were able to speak English. The way to achieve a satisfactory standard was to drill the pupils in their lines until a good, clear level of diction was reached. Asians do not have the inhibitions of Anglo-Saxons and the boys liked taking part in the stage items, and training them was quite a delight. Yvonne was a keen drama enthusiast and took an important part in helping the boys to speak up and say their lines, and also to render expert assistance with costumes.

At this point it is opportune to record the importance of the assistance and support given throughout our stay in Malaya by my wife Yvonne. She was a graduate in home science from the University of Otago, Dunedin, New Zealand, and as will be noted throughout this account was gifted and trained in a wide variety of skills, needlework being one. As Yvonne was also adept in the English language, as well as others, her contribution to the stage shows that we arranged at the various schools was outstanding. Young people are keenly appreciative of appropriate costume, and the fact that the casts went on to the stage with professional grooming gave a boost to their confidence and with it good prospects for success.

There were very few incidences during my Malayan service which I considered difficult or serious, or even vexatious, from a political or administrative aspect. However, one concerned the recitation of the *Ten Little Nigger Boys* in a Klang High School concert, I think my third and last. As stated above, the whole school from the lowest primary class to the School Certificate class made contributions, and the little boys of course usually produced a set of nursery rhymes. The programme was in every case chosen by the teacher(s) of the classes concerned, after submitting the proposals for approval to me; no item can I recollect ever refusing or even criticising. The head teacher of the Primary Department was a Tamil and the senior mistress in charge of the lowest classes an accomplished Chinese.

Rehearsals had proceeded for some weeks quite smoothly as usual, when one morning the senior master (another Tamil) came to me in some trepidation, accompanied by the primary school master, stating that a well-known Indian doctor, leader of the Hindu community, wished to make a complaint. The year was 1950, and I was duly treated to a tirade on racism for the selection of the *Ten Little Nigger Boys* on the grounds that it was a veiled attack on the Indian community, who were of course dark skinned, compared with the Chinese and light brown skinned Malays. I felt sorry for the two Indian masters, who were caught 'on the hop' even more than I was. All we could do of course was to deny the racist charge, as it was a traditional nursery rhyme known to every child who was educated in English, and withdraw the item from the programme. It was interesting as an early appearance of an attitude which has become widespread – a censorious attitude to any comment which can be interpreted as a slight on any racial group. I have often wondered since as to the fate of other items in the nursery canon, for instance, *Taffy was a Welshman, Taffy was a Thief*, and so on. Whatever the cause, there has certainly been a decline in tolerance in ordinary social life.

Our first year in Klang also saw the beginning of Yvonne's active work in teaching her subjects in the schools.[12] When it was known that Yvonne had qualifications and teaching experience in home science (or domestic science), suggestions were made by senior officers in the Education Department that she would be able to take part in this work. One of the officers was F.C. Barraclough, principal when I arrived at King Edward VII School, and later in charge of education in the State of Selangor. A start had been made pre-war in introducing domestic science in Malay girls' schools, but progress was slow, because there was a traditional opposition to formal education for girls, who numbered only a fraction of the enrolments in the boys' schools. All this changed after the war: the girls flooded into the schools, most of which had been boys' schools, and much adaptation in facilities and in staffing had to be hurriedly improvised.

So as soon as Ruth, our second daughter, was old enough to be cared for during the day by an amah, Yvonne taught home science at a girls' English school in the mornings, and held classes for Malay school women teachers in the afternoons. These classes were respectively not held every day, but Yvonne had a class of one kind each weekday, and was home at mid-day to look after Ruth's needs. Yvonne loved her work, and the cooperation and assistance she received were boundless. In the Malay classes she was assisted by some Malay school supervisors, who had some English, and assisted in devising a vocabulary for use in the teaching. As noted above, Yvonne was a good linguist, and soon had an effective programme running. It is worth mentioning that many of Yvonne's associates in these classes, teachers and students, remained her friends and kept in contact with her all her life. Of course pre-war syllabuses in domestic science, and all the equipment, had been lost, so Yvonne and her associates were in fact faced with the necessity of making a fresh start in the teaching of the subject.

A side effect of these classes was the reputation which Yvonne soon received as an expert on infant health and welfare. She had two children of her own which of course impressed her audience, and as many of the Malay teachers were married with young children, they would sometimes bring them to classes to get Yvonne's advice on ailments or diet. When we lived near Malay settlements, mothers would bring their infants round to our house, and ask the amah if 'mem' could see the children and suggest help. They always observed strict standards of politeness – it was usual to come round in the evenings, before we had our dinner, and visitors were never at all upset if 'mem' was not at home or busy.

One afternoon in June 1948, Chinese communists entered a rubber estate in Sungei Siput, Perak, took the British planter and his two European assistants from their offices and shot them dead.[13] Thus began the Emergency, a determined and well-organised effort by, it was said, the most efficient Communist Party in Asia to seize control of the country. We became only too familiar in later years with the modern apparatus of terrorism – random attacks on persons, especially British planters and tin miners and on anyone else of any race they considered an opponent. Damage to property, for example the slashing of rubber trees, and to communications, such as the derailment of trains on the railway, was common.

For the rest of that year, a group of European officials and planters, among whom I was included, were sworn-in as special constables, armed with rifles and, once every four nights in rotation, patrolled the estates and mines in the district. We never saw any 'action', but the idea was to 'show the flag' until the security forces, army and police, were able to take over the activity. Our wives met at one of the residences, often ours, awaiting our return about midnight. Of course, the thing was to get up next morning and carry on with one's duties, being careful to act as if nothing really serious was afoot. A few senior members of the High School staff agreed to take part; my recollection is that it was emphasised that this duty was voluntary – obviously an 'unwilling volunteer' would have been worse than useless. The days following a patrol seemed unusually tiring and, apart from the Emergency, everyone's normal duties were more onerous than they had been pre-war – we were still getting the country 'back on its feet'. Consequently, we were all pleased when the duty ceased at the end of the year.

The Communist guerrillas had taken to the jungles during the war, and had taken some action in harrying Japanese posts during the occupation. They refused to hand in their weapons after the war, and the authorities were in a quandary about how to tackle the problem. However, the Communists struck first, and a guerrilla war followed. The British had had experience in jungle fighting in Burma, the Australians in Papua New Guinea, and other war strategies and tactics were still fresh from Second World War actions.

For several years terrorist actions took place frequently, and no end seemed in sight. The extreme seriousness of the situation was brought home to everyone when the then High Commissioner, Sir Henry Gurney, was assassinated in October 1951 on his way to the Fraser's Hill Holiday Station. General Sir Gerald Templer was appointed Commander-in-Chief and High Commissioner from February 1952 to May 1954, and when he left the worst danger was over, but actions continued in the jungles for many years, even after the Emergency officially ended in 1960.[14]

The year 1948 was also notable in that I acquired my first motor car, again by a piece of good fortune. As mentioned earlier, the sale of motor vehicles was strictly controlled, so that those who required them to carry out their work could have the first option to buy vehicles that came into the country. The State Senior Inspector of Schools had a European inspector as his assistant, whose duties were mainly concerned with the Malay schools. He was a pre-war education officer, and was being sent on early home leave; he called on us one day, remarking that he was due to go on leave in a few weeks, and had a problem in disposing of his car, an Austin A12, which was new when he bought it about eighteen months before. Of course, we immediately said we should like to buy it. The government gave loans to officers for the purchase of motor cars, which were repaid at stated monthly amounts over an agreed term of two or three years.

My qualification for obtaining a car was my need to travel to Kuala Lumpur to instruct in the 'normal classes' on Saturday mornings, at which I was the only 'out-station' instructor who had to travel a considerable distance for this purpose. Both the purchase and a loan were approved, and for the rest of our term in Klang we had this invaluable asset. With a family, there was always the chance that one member might have to go to the hospital for medical treatment. On one occasion, we took Ruth to the hospital about midnight with a raging fever, which the able medical superintendent, an Indian, soon brought under control. The doctor said to us, 'Mr Taylor I would have come to your house, if you had phoned the hospital.' Just as important, we were able to go for drives in the cool of the evenings and visit friends. We employed a Malay driver, who stayed with us for the years when we lived in Selangor and in Tanjong Malim.

There was a friendly spirit of cooperation between the four English schools in Klang – the High School, a government school, the Methodist Anglo-Chinese boys' school, a Methodist girls' school and the convent. There were only four girls in the School Certificate class in 1949, two from each school, and the principals asked that they be allowed to attend the High School class to give them a chance of obtaining the certificate, as obviously the schools could not spare the staff to teach such a small number. The previous year, the High School class had done about average, but the results of the 1949 class were quite remarkable. About half the class reached the top Grade I certificate, and all passed with the exception of one Chinese girl. The principal of her girls' school had said that she was not up to standard for the class, but she wanted to finish her schooling in the School Certificate class, and her parents were very keen that she should do so. In every way she was a charming girl, of a good family, and she spoke beautiful English. From memory, I think she passed only the English oral examination, in English language, and perhaps Chinese. But the point of the whole arrangement was that if she completed her school course, whether she gained a certificate or not, her standing in the 'marriage market' would be enormously enhanced. I have always hoped that she attained a happy life as a result of our efforts.

When the School Certificate results appeared the following year, the High School achievement caused considerable attention among the State schools. The Governments of Singapore and the Federation had planned to raise the pre-war Raffles College, somewhat equivalent to the American liberal arts colleges with courses in Arts and Science, to a full university with the status of other similar institutions in the British Commonwealth. To supply students of sufficient calibre for the proposed university, sixth forms were established in selected schools in each State, usually the government boys' school in the State capital. Admission was decided by the results of the School Certificate Examination. When the first sixth form was established at Victoria Institution, the government boys' school in Kuala Lumpur, pupils from the High School filled a large number of the places, and I think two of the girls were included in those admitted. I had completed four years' service in June 1950, and we left for home leave to New Zealand early the next month.

Brief mention of constitutional changes in the country is appropriate at this point. There was understandably much discussion and controversy over the causes of the British defeat in Malaya in 1941–1942: one cause was stated to be the multiplicity of separate governments in a small country – the Straits Settlements including Singapore, Penang and Malacca; the nine Malay States, four of which had a federal government, as well as their individual State Councils. This gave a total of eleven largely autonomous administrations, each of which had to be approached for negotiations about war requirements, such as sites for camps, operation of military units, requisition of civil property, and so on. When the British returned in September 1945, the Colonial Office sent an official who negotiated an agreement with the sultans, guaranteeing them their status and recognition of Malay customs and the Islamic religion, but placing the entire Peninsula under one administration, a British governor ruling from Kuala Lumpur. (The new Constitution was named the Malayan Union.) When the terms of the new treaty became known, the Malays organised a national movement in opposition and refused to cooperate with the government, including boycotting the Federal Legislative Council.

A new treaty was negotiated although, as mentioned earlier, the unfortunate governor, Sir Edward Gent, was killed when his plane crashed in England on his recall for consultations. The new Constitution, Federation of Malaya, allowed for State Councils for each State and the two Settlements of Penang and Malacca, and a Federal Council in Kuala Lumpur presided over by a British High Commissioner. This Constitution took over in February 1948, when I arrived in Klang. The main change when independence came in 1957 was to convert the State Councils to elected bodies, to install an elected federal government under a prime minister, and to have a supreme ruler, equivalent to a king, elected by the nine sultans, as head of state. At the time of writing, 35 years later, the sultans in all the States have in turn served a period as supreme ruler at least once; some States have had their rulers elected more than once. When a sultan is elected to the supreme position, his heir apparent acts as regent in the State during the period of preferment.

We travelled by the *Gorgon* from Singapore to Fremantle, and by air from Perth to Sydney. The Sydney–Wellington trip was made by flying boat, which we have always thought the most interesting means of transocean travel. Unfortunately, the sea-planes were then withdrawn from the commercial air routes, and replaced by land planes, apparently on the score of economical operation. Our arrival in Wellington was greeted by a cold southerly gale, which reminded me of my departure just over four years before. We spent most of the time in Wellington with Yvonne's mother. Our Wellington doctor thought that the sudden fevers to which the girls had succumbed in Malaya might be connected with septic tonsils, so they spent two weeks in hospital recovering from an operation to remove them. It proved successful, as the girls were not troubled with this complaint afterwards.

The girls were cared for by my mother, at her request, while Yvonne and I did a motor tour of the North Island, when we managed to call on many of our friends. As we had owned the Austin A12 for over a year, we were allowed to bring it into New Zealand without paying duty, and also to sell it in New Zealand when we embarked to return to Malaya. As motor cars were still in short supply in New Zealand after the war, we should not have been able on financial grounds to purchase a vehicle to do the travelling which the imported car enabled us to do. We also took the car across Cook Strait on the ferry, and a shorter tour gave us the opportunity of seeing friends living in the South Island. We made the return trip to Singapore by air to Perth via Sydney, and then by the *Charon* via the north-west ports to Singapore, arriving in February 1951.

Chapter 5
Second tour of duty, 1951–1954

Tanjong Malim, 1951–1952

Those officials who met us as we disembarked in Singapore, and everyone who spoke to us in succeeding weeks, left us in no doubt as to the seriousness of the Emergency. The central command of the security forces kept a day-by-day catalogue of terrorist incidents of any kind. These incidents included murders of planters or tin dredge managers, and/or members of their staffs, attacks on outposts of the security forces, army or police, damage to government or private property, attacks on the railway system, and ambushes on the roads, especially where they passed through jungle country or rubber estates, which perhaps amounted to over half the total length of the roads in the Peninsula. About November 1950, the government had recalled all officers on overseas leave; I was told that I had been exempt because I was so near the normal expiration of my leave period in the January following.

When we reached Kuala Lumpur I was advised that I had been posted as 'Master of Method' at Sultan Idris Training College (for male Malay primary school teachers) 52 miles north of Kuala Lumpur, just over the border in the State of Perak. Actually I was to relieve for six months the previous holder of the post, a young Englishman, with primary school training, who would resume the position after he returned from leave. As stated earlier, most of the male education officers had as their qualifications an Honours Degree, usually in Arts, followed by a Diploma in Education and some experience in secondary school teaching, usually in the grammar schools. The expatriate officers who supervised primary schools were women, usually Froebel College trained, and entitled primary supervisors attached to the education offices in the more populous States, such as Perak and Selangor.

The Sultan Idris Training College was formed after the First World War by amalgamating two smaller colleges, one at Malacca, the other near Taiping. It had modern buildings, large and well laid-out grounds, and extensive hostels, as its 450 students from every State in the Peninsula and from Brunei were all residential. One of its distinctions was its athletics field, which boasted an entirely straight track for the 440 yards events. However, its immediate previous experience had not been happy, as there had been an outbreak of disorder including votes of no confidence by the students in the expatriate staff. A government commission had been appointed by the High Commissioner, and its recommendations had been largely implemented before I arrived. Actually, one of the three expatriates was a female Froebel graduate, who was not received well in an all-male Muslim institution.

The situation was most unfortunate, and was really an aftermath of the occupation: the officers concerned had survived their internment, but were not back to normal health, mentally or physically. Obviously they should not have been posted to an isolated rural station – Tanjong Malim is a small town containing mainly Chinese shops, surrounded by Malay villages. The total European population at that time, including planters and tin mine managers, did not number two dozen, and the people lived in isolation from each other and from the town. The country round about was very mountainous, with thick jungle. In our year there the police district had the highest incidence of terrorist attacks of any district in the Peninsula for that twelve months, of which more as we proceed.

My duties were similar to those of a Master of Method in an English training college – lecturing in teaching methods and in educational psychology, supervising the teaching practice of the students, and giving what advice and assistance appeared desirable, as required. As assistants, I had two Malay assistant lecturers, excellent men in every way, capable and enthusiastic in their work, and pleasant and cooperative colleagues. The work of the college was carried on entirely in Malay, except for some lessons in English as a second language. My lectures, given to students of each of the three years of the course, were written out by me in draft, and discussed regarding language with the staff of the Translation Bureau before delivery. I was never sure whether everyone, staff and students, was simply being polite, but these lectures appeared to 'go over' quite well.

The practice teaching was another story. There were six Malay schools attached to the college, one in Tanjong Malim and two others on the main road North, the most distant being 15 miles. Southwards, the River Bernam was crossed at the edge of the town, and you were in Selangor, where there were three schools, the most distant, also being 15 miles, being Kuala Kubu Bharu, a small town where the district office was situated, as well as the provisions shop which sold refrigerated foods, on which European households were reliant. Unfortunately, the school building, of modern construction, was requisitioned by the army in connection with Emergency operations. Classes were therefore held in the undercroft below another government building, which also gave protection from the rain. Kuala Kubu was the junction of the main road from Singapore to Penang, and a branch road across the ranges to Pahang on the east coast; at the summit was the hill station of Fraser's Hill. During my year at the college the army agreed to revert the school buildings to their intended use.

The organisation of the schools was a typical Malayan compromise. The school buildings and their sites were the property of the respective State Education Departments, so the Sultan of Perak had his photograph in three schools, the Sultan of Selangor in the other three. The States appointed and paid for a male head teacher at each school, but all the teaching and school activities, for example gardening and school games, were carried out by the college, using students as the assistant teachers. The lessons the students gave each week were planned in outline by the staff; the students were then responsible to write up their weekly lesson plan, prepare the lessons including their illustrations (which they drew themselves) and present them to their classes.

From memory, I think that each 'practice' lasted six weeks, so the staff of the schools was completely changed twice each school term. It is perhaps unnecessary to state that the standard of work in the six practising schools was well above that of even the best schools in the Peninsula. There were literally no 'poor teachers'; the students were a highly selected group from each State and, if in their first year they suffered from inexperience, their failings were immediately corrected by the staff, who spent most of our time in the schools, only attending at college at the times when we were engaged in lectures. In fact, I recall seeing very rarely an unsatisfactory lesson and only by first-year students. Occasionally a student was found to be unsuited for teaching, when he would be returned to his State of origin.

The real problem was security of the supervising staff, as terrorist incidents were frequent, at least weekly, in the Tanjong Malim district, and the Selangor area was not much better. We were under direction by the Officer Commanding the Police District (OCPD), a European with the rank of Assistant Superintendent of Police (ASP), never to give any hint of our movements while visiting the schools. Thus the only person who knew where I was going each day was Yvonne. I had the Malay driver whom I had employed in Klang, and was given a Malay police corporal armed with a rifle as escort. As stated above, I was a special constable, and provided with an army revolver, on which we were given a 'refresher course' on arrival at the station. A little later it was considered advisable for our womenfolk to be given a similar course.

Actually there was only a real chance of trouble at three schools; three were set alongside the main road, which was regularly patrolled, but three were a short distance into the jungle, with access only by a footpath. My driver and the corporal stayed by the car on the roadside while I inspected the students. One morning, the driver dashed into the school where I was at work shouting 'Sudah tembak tuan' ('There has been a shot, sir'). I ran to the car to see a bulge about the size of a tennis ball sticking out from the door on the driver's side. The unfortunate corporal had fallen asleep in the warm sunshine and accidentally fired his rifle from the inside of the car. We drove back to the police station and made the necessary report to the amused amazement of everyone on duty, from the OCPD down to the constables. The OCPD was a very able officer called Roy Henry; later in his career he became Chief Constable of the Colony of Sarawak, Police Commissioner in Fiji and then Police Commissioner in Hong Kong. That was the only 'incident' which gave me any excitement during the year at the college.

On reflection, the last statement is not quite true. As stated earlier, the friendliest relationship existed among Europeans engaged in education, at any level, and irrespective of whether employed by the government, as we were, or by the missions in the 'aided' schools. One afternoon Yvonne and I had two ladies to afternoon tea, missionaries from a school in a town over the central range in Pahang. They were on holiday, and were driving to Kuala Lumpur. Soon after we said farewell, they left on their journey, when there was a very loud explosion near our home, which was in the college compound. Everyone, including us, dashed out of our houses, and the police shot out from the police station, which was near the college entrance, to discover what had happened. Among the first on the scene was Roy Henry, the OCPD. The missionaries' car was stationary on the road nearby, having had a blow-out of its two rear tyres. The ladies had not checked their tyres for months, and they had worn so much that the tubes were showing through, yet they had travelled over a mountain road, in dangerous bandit territory for about a hundred miles without mishap! So they obtained new tyres and moved on their way.

TKT with Mark 1951

Mark was born in that year, and we had arranged a baptism with the Anglican vicar in Kuala Lumpur, who came and stayed with us that night. The ceremony and reception was held in our house, attended by all the European community in the district who could come. I remember the pile of weapons, mainly revolvers and their holsters and belts, which the planters and police deposited under the watchful eye of a constable inside the house while the company was present. Nothing untoward occurred during the afternoon, but that night at about 2 a.m. there was an explosion from behind the house where the River Bernam flowed near the college. The Communists had thrown hand grenades into the police post at the river ford, killing the two police on duty. These incidents give some impression of daily life at this time, as the Emergency could affect people not having a direct connection with the military situation.

The Translation Bureau was an office of the Federal Department of Education, which was located at the college for convenience. As the title indicates, the staff were basically concerned with preparing textbooks for use in Malay schools; textbooks which were usually adaptations of English primary texts published with the approval and cooperation of the publishing houses. The staff were Malay male officials, two or three of them, who were excellent in their command of English and Malay, and expert as translators. Of course, the translators often used the advice of college staff in their work, as well as assisting me in preparing lectures or official reports, all of which were done in Malay.

On Saturdays, when we had no college duties, we would often go into Kuala Lumpur, 52 miles south, to shop and to visit friends. All our domestic needs, except provisions, had to be obtained from Kuala Lumpur, the nearest town to our station; we made the trip to consult the doctor or dentist, as well as to obtain clothing and other personal supplies. After our son Mark was born in July, Yvonne did not accompany me on these trips, and I made the journey with the driver to obtain what our family needed, sometimes to execute commissions for other Europeans, and also to consult government departments on behalf of the college, at the request of the principal, the college being a federal responsibility. In October of that year, I had proceeded south of Kuala Kubu on my way to Kuala Lumpur, when I was met about mid-morning by the official car carrying the High Commissioner and Lady Gurney; the car quite obvious from the two flags, the Union Jack and the Federation flag flying on the bonnet of the car. There were two police motorcycle escorts ahead, and an armoured vehicle behind the official car. During my visits that day to the government offices, I gained the impression that the prevailing mood was not one of confidence – perhaps there had been a number of serious incidents in the previous week.

I returned to Tanjong Malim about 5 p.m., without incident, and was met at the entrance to the college grounds, which were surrounded by a barbed wire fence, by the chief clerk, a Malay, looking very sombre. He asked me, 'Have you heard the news?', which of course I hadn't. I was then told that the High Commissioner had been assassinated in an ambush while proceeding up the winding road to the Fraser's Hill Station. As the point where I met the High Commissioner's party was only a short distance from the junction on the main road where the side road to the holiday station branched off, I have always been fairly sure that I was the last European, certainly the last government officer, to see Sir Henry Gurney alive. In brief, the result was to redouble efforts both in Malaya and in

London to bring the Emergency under control. It so happened that about the same date Winston Churchill returned to office, and the new British Government gave the Malayan situation top priority. After most careful and extensive discussion, General Sir Gerald Templer was appointed High Commissioner and Commander-in-Chief, and arrived in Malaya on 7 February 1952, the day after the death of King George VI. This date and the event will be referred to later in the narrative.

No more positive indication of the predicament of the country can be given than by stating it proved impossible for some months to transfer me to my next posting, because, quite literally, no house could be found to accommodate my family and me in the State of Selangor. I have said that my term as Master of Method was in fact a relieving appointment. After about six months the regular occupant of the post arrived back from leave and took over his former duties from me. Under the system of home leave explained earlier, the roster of those leaving and returning, and of their postings, was compiled months in advance, and any changes to the roster would have a 'domino effect' on other officers' arrangements. I had been designated as headmaster at the High School, Kajang, about 20 miles south of Kuala Lumpur, on the expiration of my stay in Tanjong Malim – but could not make the transfer because there was nowhere to live! I mentioned earlier that the army had requisitioned the Kuala Kubu Malay school – they had also hired many residences normally occupied by civil government officers.

When I left duty at the college as Master of Method, the only place for us to go was in some rooms at the Rest House. Yvonne and I, our three children, one an infant, two amahs and a driver made some demands on the available accommodation in a small Rest House in a small town. With the cooperation of the Rest House staff (Chinese) we fared quite well with our meals and, as always, Yvonne did wonders in looking after us in other respects, for instance in keeping the servants occupied and as comfortable as possible. Kajang was one of the most troubled towns in the country, hence the security forces had taken every available building, including the headmaster's residence at the school. As Kajang was such a short distance from Kuala Lumpur on the main road, we could have lived in a house in the capital, or in the adjacent area, and thence I could have commuted daily to work. But the army had made similar demands on the available accommodation in Kuala Lumpur. I had government authority to rent any house which Yvonne and I thought remotely suitable – but there were none, all avenues having been explored.

Kate and Ruth 1952, Tanjong Malim

A government officer, transferred to Johore, was vacating a private house, and advised me before he left the house. I visited the owner, a Chinese magnate, in his fine modern office. He gave me a courteous reception, and told me he would give me an answer next day. When he informed me that he was sorry he had let the house to someone else, I assumed a commercial executive who would be able to outbid the rate the government was willing to pay. I should mention that the monthly rent which the government offered me was almost equal to my monthly salary, so there was no question that a reasonable effort was made by the government to house its officers.

We were indeed well off in Tanjong Malim; the hotels in Kuala Lumpur were full of government officials and army officers, for whom no housing was available. There were a large number of families in these hotels in cramped and restricted conditions. As a result, a programme of building temporary accommodation was put in hand, and the situation improved in the following years. However, there was no house available for us, and so I was one headmaster which the Kajang High School never had! The school functioned under an Asian acting headmaster, but it had not fared well after the occupation, and the Emergency had caused further problems and lowered morale.

My term as a supernumerary officer, and our stay in the Tanjong Malim Rest House, ended in an unexpected manner. One evening there was a ring on the Rest House phone, and the supervisor said the call was for me. It was the Director of Education, L.D. Whitfield, asking me if I would go down to Johore Bahru, at the southernmost part of the Peninsula, to take over as headmaster of the English College at that town in order to relieve the incumbent, who had had to resign from the Service on medical grounds.

During the last months of my stay in Tanjong Malim, I had no regular duties attached to a position on the staff. In the intervals of performing those extra tasks assigned to me, I had the opportunity of furthering my study of the Malay language and literature, history and antiquities, in other words of attempting the Standard III Malay Examination, the final and optional stage. Officers were required to apply for permission to take the examination and if you succeeded within a stated period, from memory three years, a bonus of about one month's salary was paid as a reward. Of course, the college was the best location for the study, as it had a highly qualified staff, and also a library of works in Malay and about the Malays. The staff of the Translation Bureau were always ready to assist with problems of translation, from and into Malay. As a result of my first attempt at the examination, I succeeded in passing most of the papers, and had to do further work in conversation and in reading the Jawi (Arabic) manuscript writing, of which more later. One of the set works was an account by a Malay on Stamford Raffles' staff, one Munshi (i.e. teacher) Abdullah, of his travels accompanying Raffles on his official journeys in Singapore and around the Peninsula. Abdullah was similar in his relationship to Raffles as Boswell was to Dr Johnson, and his account is one of the most important sources, both for the life of Raffles and for conditions in the area at the beginning of the nineteenth century.

Leaving Tanjong Malim also meant that we had to say farewell to our driver, Baba, and his family. As Selangor Malays, they were prepared to go just across the border into Perak, but to go to the furthest southern tip of the Peninsula, to a strange land, Johore, was a very different story. There were differences in dialect between the various States, though generally they could understand each other, in costume and in social conditions, much as, say, the inhabitants of various regions in England have marked characteristics. Actually, the family would have come with us to Johore, but mother-in-law 'put her foot down', and back to Klang they went. One thing I learnt by living in the country was that the mother-in-law is the real ruler of Asia, in very important ways; I was always quite sure that the

Chinese magnate, to whom I applied to rent his house, had been overruled by his mother-in-law. And it must be remembered that in the East there is no old age pension or social security, and the best asset an old woman can have is a reliable and useful son-in-law as a support in her old age, with her daughter's services added for good measure. To do the women justice, they earned their keep by supervising and caring for the young children when the mothers were down at the river washing, or at the market obtaining food. So I drove down to Johore Bahru by myself, and Yvonne, the two amahs and the children would follow as soon as I had obtained quarters.

This account would be seriously deficient if I omitted to pay a tribute to my driver, Baba, who gave excellent service the whole time that he was with me. But over and above the duties which he was employed to do, he gave me his unhesitating and ready loyalty in what were difficult circumstances. Malaya is a 'dream scenario' for guerrillas or terrorists. The jungle comes right to the side of the roads wherever there is no cultivation or habitation and the untilled areas are covered with long grasses or undergrowth, just as effective as the jungle in hiding an ambush.

When on our visits to the schools, Baba drove on, outwardly unconcerned, but all the while looking for any suspicious movement in the vegetation, while I did the same on my side. If there was a hint of confrontation, our instructions were to drive on quickly regardless. To give an incident as an example, one of the planters in Tanjong Malim came across some bandits on his way down from his bungalow to the main road. In a flash, he reversed and drove at top speed up the road to the house, where he telephoned the police. The house was, of course, surrounded by a high fence, and there were several guards who were capable of warding off an attack, especially as the bandits would normally have to advance to the house some yards in the open. As far as I remember, we did not see Baba and his family again.

English College, Johore Bahru and Johore Education Office, 1952–1954

The distance from Tanjong Malim to Johore Bahru is about 300 miles, a long day's drive. As was customary, I left Tanjong Malim at first light, about 6 a.m., and, after passing through Selangor, stopped for breakfast at the Rest House in Seremban, the capital of Negri Sembilan, the next State south. Getting out of the car, on the way to the Rest House, I saw the newspaper handbill 'King George VI dies'. It was the 7th of February 1952, on which day General Sir

Gerald Templer arrived to assume duty as High Commissioner and Commander-in-Chief, accompanied by his deputy, a senior colonial servant, Sir Donald McGillivray. The main road south passes through the centre of Johore, along which there were several bandit-infested villages. I had therefore been advised to take the coast road, and had the experience of crossing the wide rivers at Muar and Batu Pahat by the ferries – large barges towed across the river by launches. I reached the Rest House, Johore Bahru, without incident just after dark, about 7 p.m., where I had dinner. I spoke to the State chief education officer, and we arranged to meet Tony Hill at the English College for the 'take over' next morning.

English College staff about May 1952

It will already have been evident that the Emergency and its incidents had a material effect on the lives of all of us, whatever the official position in which we worked. At the time of my transfer to Johore, this State was considered overall to have worse problems regarding the Emergency than any other State. On my car journey south to Johore, as recommended, I deviated to the coastal road on which the two main towns, Muar and Batu Pahat, are situated. Each is at the mouth of a wide river, passable by a motor drawn barge. But the behaviour of the children was the most interesting thing; they played very quietly, contrary to the normal behaviour of children everywhere; no laughter or lively chatter, and no running around in games of chase. One felt that there was a brooding threat hanging over the lives of these people, which they saw no prospect of dis-solving. As noted above, the coastal region was relatively free of incidents, but the seriousness of the general situation had its effect on the atmosphere of daily living, wherever one happened to be.

As arranged, on the morning after my arrival, I made my way to the English College, and took over my duties as headmaster from A.H. Hill, in the company of A.F. Hunter, the chief education officer. Tony Hill was one of the leading Malay scholars in the Government Service as a whole, not only in the Education Department. My impression of him was of a very tired man, to the point of being worn out; he had been in charge of education in Kelantan, on the Siam border ('Thailand' came later), where the population is almost entirely Malay, and its politics devious. He received us cordially, and his conversation gave some indication of his eminence as a scholar. I am sorry to have to add another report of a tragic end to a career. Tony settled in Sydney, where he obtained a post as a senior lecturer in the Department of Malay and Indonesian Studies at the University of Sydney. A few years after his arrival in Sydney, he was on study leave in Indonesia, when his Garuda aircraft collided with the side of a mountain, with the loss of all on board.

The next months were occupied by my getting to know the school, its staff and problems, and familiarising myself with the State of Johore and its characteristics. Johore was pre-war the oldest of the Unfederated Malay States, having been associated with Britain since Singapore was founded in 1819. The principle of British control was in essence the same as that in the Federated Malay States, that the sultan would accept the advice of the British Advisor on all matters except on the Muslim religion and Malay customs. But Johore, under the very independent-minded and autocratic Sultan Ibrahim, adopted an individual attitude on many things – for instance the 'FMS Railway',[15] which connected Singapore with the Siam railway, in Johore was officially the 'Johore State Railway'. The standard of government services was not as good as that in the FMS, but better than in the four northern States which passed from the control of Siam to that of Britain in 1909. The relative state of progress was really a matter of time – British involvement was about 30 years after that of the Federated Malay States, which means that modern development dated back only about 40 years at the Japanese occupation. Thus the part of the population middle aged in 1952 could remember most of the changes which had taken place. Indeed the sultan under whom the changes had taken place was still alive, but living in England. His son was the regent in our time; Johore had only formally accepted British guidance with the appointment of a British General Advisor in 1914.

The first step on my arrival was, of course, to arrange for my family to come down to Johore Bahru from Tanjong Malim. Again, there was a shortage of official accommodation, and when the family arrived in Johore the only course available was to stay in a hotel in Singapore, from where I commuted daily the distance of 20 miles or so, across the Singapore Island and to the college along the main road beside the Straits of Johore. Of course, this was very expensive to the government, and after about two weeks we were assigned a pleasant modern two-storey house on the slopes of the hill on which the government offices were situated. Apparently, local Malay officials were entitled to government quarters, for which they paid a low rent. The 'locals', after some years' service, acquired their own houses, which they rented for extra income, continuing to occupy the government houses themselves. So it was possible to remove the Malay and his family quickly in order to house the Taylors with great benefit to the government expenditure account. The college was about two miles from the house along the Straits of Johore, by a pleasant tree-lined stretch of the main highway to Kuala Lumpur. After a few miles it turned north and ran up the centre of the State to connect in turn with the highway to the States of the north.

The English College was different from the schools in Taiping and Klang, which were 'continuous stream' schools, from the lowest primary class to School Certificate, as it was composed of secondary classes only. The organisation of the boy's English schools in Johore Bahru is the only one of its kind I have seen anywhere. Young boys aged 6 plus started at a primary school, where they stayed for four years; the next four years were spent at a middle school, at a different site, whence they passed on to the college for the four years leading to School Certificate. The headmaster of the college was ranked as a 'superscale' post, a grade below Taiping, but a grade above Klang, which was a 'timescale' post. The principal of Sultan Idris Trainee College was on a still higher grade. As I was acting in the post, they paid me the salary while I was employed as headmaster, but I reverted to my ordinary rank and salary when I ceased duty there, and went later as Inspector of Schools to the State Education Office.

The University of Malaya, as stated earlier, had been established in Singapore in 1949, by combining the pre-war College of Medicine and Raffles College, similar to a liberal arts college. Building on this nucleus, the university was proceeding to add to the courses offered and to expand its enrolment. As mentioned earlier, this required an upgrading of entrance qualifications of students, which for British universities was then the Higher School Certificate, taken two years after the School Certificate. As the university, unlike the schools, followed the northern academic year (to facilitate the employment of staff from these universities) the expedient was instituted of a sixth-form course following the School Certificate, consisting of four terms, that is, one complete year, January to December, plus the following term, when an entrance examination was held. The successful students entered university the following September. The sixth-form class for Johore State was established in the college, consisting of boys and girls from any of the English schools, those students living outside Johore Bahru boarding in the town. Classes had been established in some centres, such as Kuala Lumpur, from 1950, but the class of 1952 which I met at the college on my arrival was the first in Johore. It consisted of about twenty students, of all races, of whom about four were girls.

Another complication arising from the disharmony between the northern and southern educational years was the late arrival of the results of the School Certificate Examination held the previous December, which did not reach Malaya till March. As these results provided the criteria for admission to a sixth form (a Grade II minimum was required), the students were admitted in January on the estimated results supplied by the schools of origin. There was also the performance of the students in class to be considered, so on either count, or both, a final decision was made at the end of the first term in April. The final number admitted was about fifteen, including three girls. From memory, the students were required to sit three papers, a general paper and an English paper, which were compulsory, and a third paper from the other subjects – mathematics, history, etc. – chosen according to the students' intended university course. I followed my predecessor in taking the general paper. Tony Hill had left me a book which described the great religions, with their historical background – we had at least one pupil of each of the Christian, Muslim, Buddhist and Hindu religions – and we discussed current history, of Malaya especially, but also that of other countries of East Asia, and world events which impinged on Malaya.

As has been indicated, the University of Malaya was a new and fledgling, or developing, institution which was very restricted in two ways – in the number of students it could accommodate and still more by the number of courses it could offer. A very important aspect of the work of the English schools was the opportunity they gave to children of the wealthier families to go overseas for university education, at first mainly to Britain, but in my time quite extensively also to other English-speaking countries – Australia, Canada, the United States and New Zealand, my guess is roughly in that order.

From 1885 the Government of the Straits Settlements, and from 1901 the Federated Malay States, granted one or two expensive scholarships each year, awarded on an examination, to students for university courses in Britain, usually to Oxford or Cambridge. These students, on qualifying, returned home and produced a succession of distinguished citizens in various occupations – medicine, law, the civil service – which gave the country a good contact with the outside world when independence came in 1957. In later years the scholarships were awarded to graduates of the College of Medicine and Raffles College for post-graduate study to the United Kingdom.

The previous paragraph leads to the explanation that the sixth forms established in Malaya had an important function in preparing students to take the Cambridge Higher School Certificate Examination, in addition to the University of Malaya Entrance Examination. The examinations were taken in the Decembers preceding and following the Entrance Exam. Of course, children of wealthier families went straight to the United Kingdom, whether or not they gained admission to the University of Malaya, but students who aimed to study locally also entered for subjects at Higher School Certificate, which gave them an added qualification, as well as additional experience in study and in coping with examinations. The Higher School Certificate worked on a system of credits, varying between advanced (major) and subsidiary units; to obtain a Higher School Certificate the candidate had to pass in sufficient units to reach a set total, and a stated number of advanced units had to be included. If a student aimed to do an arts, science or economics degree, of course the subject(s) in which he intended to specialise would be taken as major units.

My share in the teaching of the sixth form, in addition to classes preparing for the general paper, was to assist in English teaching, and by request of the students, the Higher School Certificate subsidiary paper in the history of East Asia. By this year I had completed most of the government Standard III Malay Examination, something like honours level at a university of the British type. The syllabus included China, Japan and all the countries of South East Asia, but the actual examination paper made provision for a selection of the areas studied, so we did the history of China, Japan and, of course, Malaya.

Here it may be opportune to record my fate with the Standard III Malay Examination. As stated above, at the end of the previous year at Tanjong Malim I had passed nearly all the examination, excepting the conversation test and the Malay manuscript translation test. The latter consisted, put simply, of a piece of nearly indecipherable scrawl in the Arabic script by a Kampong (Village) Malay, which the candidate had to decipher and translate. This test had usually been taken by administrative officers, most of whom were employed, at least over some years, in district offices (as district officers), many of which were in remote districts – on the smaller stations the DO was often the only European official. Especially when British administration was first established, the officials most of the time were occupied in talking to the local people, and quite often in receiving handwritten letters in indifferently legible script. The DOs of course became quite expert in reading these letters. I remember a colleague, who also had failed this test, saying he took the paper to a senior MCS[16] official, who thereupon read it straight off as if it were in print.

Anyhow, I wrote in to the chief examiner pointing out that most of us never saw this illegible script, as our school pupils wrote in beautiful copperplate. The test was revised to a more straightforward handwriting; I passed the examination, but too late to get my bonus.

The lessons which I took with the sixth form were not the only ones which concerned me as headmaster, because, in brief, the school was desperately understaffed, even by the standard of the conditions prevailing in the country at the time. As noted above, Johore had not had the length of time under British guidance of the Federated Malay States, resulting in the lack of a tradition of English-educated people which had developed in those States. Second, Johore had no single large central town as the capital, where the leading facilities, including schools, tended to be concentrated. As I arrived during the first term, I let the school 'run' until the end of term, when the normal class tests were held, and then held a general staff meeting to decide on measures for improvement.

Some progress was made by reallocating subjects in classes to teachers qualified and keen to teach them – for some reason unknown to me the existing timetable had been drafted in a mechanical manner, simply dividing the teaching periods to achieve an equal number of teaching periods per teacher, except of course in the School Certificate class, where the teaching to be effective must be done by specialists. Teachers who were, say, Raffles College graduates offered to take extra periods in their subjects, allowing teachers with Normal Teaching Certificates to take subjects in the lower classes. It was considered a good thing for the headmaster to take lessons in the classes at all levels in the school, but as far as possible, I 'filled in' with those classes where there were 'gaps', taking English and history lessons where these were left vacant. In addition, the wife of the British Advisor, an Oxford honours graduate in languages, offered to assist, and came for part of each school day. With the adoption of these expedients morale was immediately boosted, and accordingly the whole tone and efficiency of the school improved greatly.

A most serious disadvantage had to be surmounted by the departure in May on transfer to Hong Kong of the only European Colonial Service staff member, who was the history specialist. As his replacement did not arrive till the third term in September, these lessons also had to be 'covered' in the interim. I took the senior history classes, but many of the other periods went into abeyance, teachers available in their 'free' periods taking the classes for extra work in the subjects in which they were competent.

My wife did no teaching while we were in Johore; from memory, there was no demand for a home economics teacher – just as well, as we had three young children, including a baby boy. To add to the exigencies of life, I was asked to take part in the provision of normal classes by correspondence. There were about six towns, besides Johore Bahru, in the State with English schools. In Johore, the seriousness of the Emergency had one effect, that travel on the roads was dangerous, and students could not travel in safety to a centre where normal classes were formerly held. My subject, as it had been in Selangor, was the principles and practice of teaching, so I converted my lectures into written assignments, to which the students responded by returning answers to the questions set each week. Once again I was indebted to Yvonne for invaluable assistance; she typed the Gestetner masters from which the lessons were duplicated, and her own English being quite outstanding, she also acted as a subeditor to my work, throughout her life, which saved me very much time in proof-reading. The usual Saturday morning normal classes were held at the college for Johore Bahru students. Looking back on my working life, there is no doubt that my first year at the college was the most strenuous in all my career.

By the time August arrived, we felt that a holiday was much needed, and I obtained local leave to go to the holiday resort of Port Dickson, Negri Sembilan, where we had gone while living in Klang. The girls, at 5 and 4 years old, were very happy to spend as much time as possible on the glorious beach, and Mark, just over a year, was now walking and interested in exploring wherever he happened to be. I mentioned above how the repressed and listless behaviour of the children on my trip down to Johore indicated to me how heavily the Emergency was bearing on the population. No greater contrast can be imagined between the demeanour of the population in February and what we saw while passing through the same towns and villages in August. It was quite remarkable how the children, at any rate, had thrown off the fear and depression so general six months before. They played with the usual carefree abandon common to normal children anywhere; the whole of Templer's term as High Commissioner was concerned with relentless action against the terrorists, but it was quite unmistakable that the common people had every confidence that the threat would finally be overcome. Such is the transformation in attitude which a leader of real ability is able to inspire. Our holiday was the more effective through seeing the change in attitude now evident in the community.

The following year life continued much the same, except that the college functioned on regular lines, without the stresses occasioned by the problems of 1952. The first university entrance examination in the college was held at the end of the first term; this was made memorable for me by a Malay man – the students were still well over the age of 18, following the 'break' of the Japanese occupation – who contracted influenza on the first of the three-day examination. Obtaining what medical advice I could to help him, I called at the house where he boarded before each paper, and returned him to his lodgings afterwards, and he managed to complete the examination in this way. He came from a remote village in the north of the State, and was the weakest student in the class, and we, the staff, had little hope of his passing under the circumstances. However, when the results were published in the following term, all our students had passed for admission to the university, one of the few classes in the country to achieve 100 per cent. The chief education officer granted us a half-holiday, a customary celebration when a school achieved this result, usually with the School Certificate classes. As the college had never achieved a similar distinction before, the effect on the further increase in morale was marked.

There was a happy sequel to the sick Malay student's success in the entrance examination. He duly obtained his degree at the university, was appointed to the Malayan Civil Service, the government Administrative Service, and before we left the country, Yvonne and I received an invitation to his marriage, into an aristocratic family in Kuala Lumpur, which was celebrated by a large gathering.

An incident which caused some amusement among the staff occurred also in my first year. The sultan had given permission for a 'Grand Prix' to be held with the route passing through the main streets of Johore Bahru. Those concerned with public safety, the administrative officers and the police especially, were in some trepidation about controlling the crowds of onlookers. The first decision made was, quite properly, that all the schools were to open as usual, with suitable penalties for anyone who 'wagged it' on the day. Accordingly, I issued instructions that all class registers were to be marked when the school opened, and sent to me immediately, from which I made a list of absentees, with the further notice that all those boys were to report to me next morning. Of course, a few parents had written a falsehood stating that their son was ill, but seventeen were left (I remember the number) and were promptly caned. I suppose this was as many as I had to punish in the rest of my career.

Another curious arrangement of the school was the employment of two contractors in the school tuck shop, apparently to introduce competition. One of these men absented himself, to get the advantage of larger profits at a wayside stall selling food to the Grand Prix spectators. The half hour break at about 11 a.m. is the time for the main meal of Asians, so about half the school had to go hungry. The contractor was therefore dismissed forthwith, which pleased the staff, as he was not liked. At the time, the staff dubbed the incident as 'the morning of the long knives'.

A posting in the Government Service to Johore Bahru was sought-after, for the obvious reason that it placed you in what was geographically a suburb of Singapore. As the distance by road across the island was 17 miles, the distance to be travelled from one's home in Johore Bahru to a destination in Singapore would only be about 20 miles. Accordingly, a family living in Johore Bahru would shop locally only for food; all else would be obtained in Singapore, where the prices were lower, partly because Singapore was a 'Free Port'. On the way home you stopped at the customs post on the boundary, and would have to pay duty, where applicable, on all items purchased in Singapore, except what could be worn. So you wore your new pair of shoes, jacket or dress; it was not uncommon for women to wear their new evening frock through customs. The variety of entertainment and social facilities available in Singapore was obviously much greater than was available anywhere in the Federation. There was indeed a European Club in Johore Bahru, which held a club night on Saturdays, and also during public holidays. Otherwise Singapore was the social centre for the European community in the district. In addition to State government officers, there was a large army establishment, and across the Straits were the naval workshops, many of whose British staff lived in Johore Bahru. There was a school in the navy base for the children of men in any of the services, which also admitted children of civil government officers.

English College school sports 1954; Mark aged 3 sitting just behind TKT

Two years had passed since my arrival at the English College; the 1954 school year had begun and enrolments and the timetable had been finalised to enable the year's programme to proceed. One afternoon I was working in the office, listening to the conversation, in Malay, of some senior Malay boys outside the office, whose voices I recognised. After a few minutes a new voice, speaking excellent Malay, joined the group. Interested, I went outside and met 'Tinggi' Rees (Tinggi is Malay for 'tall'), who was to succeed me when I went on leave. He had spent most of his career, at his own request, in the east coast State of Trengganu, and was recognised as one of the leading Malay scholars in the Government Service. Indeed, he was often called upon to vet important official documents in Malay before they were promulgated. After nearly 30 years in the Service his retirement was approaching, so he was given the post as headmaster of the college to give him a superscale salary on which his retirement pension would be calculated.

Thus it happened that my last few months of the tour were spent as Inspector of Schools in the State Education Office, Johore, which coincided with Sir Gerald Templer's last months as High Commissioner. My transfer was fortuitous in several ways, first and immediately as a change from the strenuous grind of work at the college. By now the chief education officer was R.W. Watson Hyatt, a delightful chief to work for, but sadly a very sick man suffering from a nervous complaint which affected his balance and therefore his ability to walk. His wife brought him to office daily, and called to take him home at the end of office hours. The improvement mentioned earlier in the 'security' situation had so far much advanced that it was now possible in daylight hours, and subject to certain precautions, for government officers to go on tour on inspecting duties. However, it was not possible for Watson Hyatt to travel, so he asked me to act as his deputy, and call on schools which had problems of such a kind as to be more easily overcome by consultation on the spot.

The English schools were directly administered in the States by the chief education officer, and, other than those in Johore Bahru, there were two in west coast towns, Batu Pahat and Muar, the largest towns and both substantial ports, two in Kluang and Segamat on the main highway in the centre of the State, and two more in Kota Tinggi and Mersing on the east coast. I visited all these towns at least once: in Kluang there was also a convent school where the European staff were a lively and charming bunch of Spanish nuns. Most of the matters discussed with school principals concerned school buildings, many of which needed extensions to cope with the larger enrolments, and staffing shortages arising from the same cause. The experience was useful to me, as in the following year I was to go to Pahang on the east coast just north of Johore, as chief education officer. Sadly, Watson Hyatt had to leave the Service on medical grounds soon after I went on leave, and died in England only a few months afterwards.

Recreation leave: June 1954–February 1955

We went on long leave in the first week of June 1954, after another long tour of over three years. The expatriate officers were consulted about the dates of their departure on leave, two considerations being paramount: the family concerns about placement of children in school, and the very desirable opportunity of enjoying at least a part of the summer in the country concerned. By leaving in June, including time spent on the voyage, we had over seven months which gave us until January in New Zealand. The leave periods, which despite their length passed all too quickly, allowed us to spend some time with our families, visit friends with the aid of the car we brought with us from Malaya, and allow the girls some months at a New Zealand school, as they were 6 and 7 years of age respectively. Up to this point their education had entirely been Yvonne's work, as there were no pre-school classes in Johore. The age of admission to a government English school was 6 years on the first of January; Kate was able to attend the convent school a few months before we left Johore, but Ruth, to her chagrin, being a year younger, had to continue with 'mum's school'.

On our way back to Malaya at the end of this leave, both girls entered St Hilda's Girls' School, Perth, Western Australia. Their successful school career was a positive indication of how well Yvonne had provided the basis for smooth transition to their formal education. The two girls had been registered for admission to St Hilda's when Kate was a year old; on mentioning the birth of Ruth, the school advised us to apply for both to be admitted at the one time, so Ruth was duly registered when she was a few months old. On our return journey in February 1955, we arranged to spend a week in Perth at the time the schools reopened at the beginning of the school year. We accordingly deposited the girls on the day specified, which was a few days before their birthdays, which fell on successive days the following week. The boarders had arrangements for the observance of their birthdays; we left their presents with the housemistress, who showed us where the girls would sleep. They were the two youngest in the house that year, and I remember leaving as they lined up for their evening meal, at the end of the line. The girls boarded for six years until we took up residence in Perth in 1960. The next day we sailed from Fremantle in the *Charon* and proceeded to Kuala Lumpur.

Chapter 6
Third tour of duty, 1955–1957

Kuala Lumpur: February–May 1955

On arrival, I was informed that I was to serve in the Federal Education Department as assistant director of education, 'C' – the director was the senior official, and there was a deputy director, and three assistant directors, 'A', 'B' and 'C' respectively. This really meant that I was the third and junior secretary to the department. I had a portfolio of duties, one of which I remember being the oversight of departmental publications, that is, the translations of texts used in Malay schools, which emanated from the Translation Bureau situated in Sultan Idris Training College, Tanjong Malim. My correspondence was mainly with the publishers and on occasion with the Colonial Office, London, and with chief education officers, signing my name over 'Director of Education'. As it was understood that I was merely to 'keep the seat warm' in that office pending my relieving the principal of the college in Tanjong Malim, I was not given projects of which the negotiations would carry on for some time, and in any case I was careful to have my important memos overseen by a relevant senior officer before acting further.

An amusing circumstance, which possibly can only arise in a close-knit service whose members are frequently interchanged, as we were, arose when I addressed letters and instructions to the principal, Sultan Idris Training College, which I knew I should reply to, or carry out myself. As I have indicated, my portfolio included some functions of the college at Tanjong Malim. The director remarked that in the circumstances I should have to be watched, as I might be favouring the college with extra provision of equipment and grants! This was of course impossible, as all financial dealings were controlled by one finance officer. Later on, I shall comment on the running of the Malayan Government Service. I have always thought it remarkable that even with the battering it received under the Japanese occupation, and the severe losses to its personnel by death and deprivations, the Service functioned so efficiently and reliably during my time in the country. There was, needless to say, the perennial problem of corruption, including the petty kind among junior clerks or hospital attendants, for instance, and this was the target of one of Templer's several campaigns to improve the standard of public service behaviour. But throughout the 'Emergency,' all branches of Government Service continued to function, and the standard of service improved each year, as the effects of the Japanese occupation were rectified, and as the number of terrorist incidents decreased. While in Kuala Lumpur, we were given quarters in a 'chalet' provided as temporary accommodation for government officers.

Tanjong Malim: May–November 1955

Our second period at Tanjong Malim, while I relieved R.A. Goodchild on leave for six months, was uneventful, and perhaps the quietest of my entire career in Malaya. The college appeared to be running very smoothly, the working atmosphere and relationships of staff and students very good. The only matter of any note was the fact that the Malayan Scout Congress was to be held at the college during the August vacation, at which the High Commissioner as chief scout was to address the gathering and stay at the principal's residence. Accordingly, Yvonne and I had the High Commissioner to stay overnight, and we held a dinner that evening for the senior scout officials and local dignitaries. The proceedings went off without incident. As a security precaution, the High Commissioner, Sir Donald McGillivray, made the trip from Kuala Lumpur by helicopter, which landed and took off from the college hockey field. The pilot took Mark, then aged four, into the 'copter which pleased our son mightily.

The first national elections to elect members of the Federal Legislative Council were also held while we were at Tanjong Malim, again without incident of any kind. As mentioned earlier, in 1951 this district had the highest number of terrorist attacks of any in the country; the month after Templer's arrival, there was a very bad ambush, in which the British district officer, the British engineer and several police were killed on their way to repair a water main, previously blown up by the same terrorists. The town was put on 22-hour curfew, and a house to house distribution of forms demanded information on the communists. The replies were collected in sealed boxes, opened personally by Templer himself, and arrests made. All these things were events of the past by the time we stayed in Tanjong Malim, and we noted the entirely different atmosphere in the town from that in our previous term.

In the meantime, another European officer in the Education Service had had to retire on medical grounds. He had been chief education officer at Pahang, and I was asked to assume duty in that office when the Goodchilds returned from leave. So once again, as at Klang and at Johore Bahru, I had an unexpected posting due to the medical unfitness of an officer while serving in a post.

Pahang: November 1955–April 1957

We arrived in Kuantan, on the east coast, the State capital, in November, just as the monsoon season was about to begin. The Malay Peninsula is within the region where a monsoon effect causes variation in the annual climate, but it is only on the edge of the area. On the western side there is on average a heavier rainfall from November to February, but it is not really very noticeable, as heavy showers are experienced every few days, or daily, throughout the year. But the east coast does experience a monsoon season, regular in its appearance but varying in intensity. Shortly after our arrival the monsoon set in, as eerie an experience of the ways of nature as I have ever encountered. The 'normal' downpours usually take place in the afternoons, anywhere in the Peninsula or Singapore, and for a few days after we came to Kuantan the rainfall was heavier and more frequent than usual. Then one day the rain started with a steady downpour of tropical intensity, the sky took on a steely grey appearance, and the rain just never stopped. It was heavy continuously not lessening or becoming heavier at any time, just this monotonous and steady pour. The dull sound of rushing water, effectively blotted out familiar sounds – no birds or animals could be heard, and traffic on the road went by with a distant murmur.

The Government of Pahang every year sent out a circular detailing the precautions to be taken to prepare for a period of up to four months when transport might be difficult or unreliable, or even impossible. The main thing was to ensure that sufficient supplies were stored to last through the monsoon period. The arrangements had been made in October, before my arrival, but an obvious first task was to familiarise myself with the problems and the expedients used to maintain government services. Many of the Malay villages were situated on the banks of rivers, and often the school ground was the only level cleared area in the village. The monsoon instruction for the schools was quite simple – a school was closed for the period when its grounds were under water. The buildings were of course erected on tall piles high enough to keep them above normal flood levels. As may be imagined, a monsoon flood was not regarded by the pupils or teachers as an unmitigated hardship!

Pahang is by far the largest State in the country in terms of area, and the most mountainous, so its population was rather less than that of Malacca, the second smallest State. All things considered, we looked back on our 18 months in Pahang as the most enjoyable and interesting of our time in the country. Three things have been mentioned, the size of the State, its climate influenced by the monsoon, and its sparse population, which was located in small areas adjacent to the six towns of any size, separated by long distances along narrow and winding roads in contrast to conditions usual elsewhere in the Peninsula. Much of the Malay population lived in villages on the river banks, and the resulting difficulty in communication had a number of consequences for the government and the life of the people. But a further circumstance, unique in Malaya, was the move of the State capital, about six months before our arrival, from the western towns of Kuala Lipis and Raub, to Kuantan, the port on the east coast. No other instance is known to me of a capital being divided between two towns. The reason for this was simply that none of the towns in the west had sufficient level land to accommodate the government buildings. The State Education Office was one of those which had been located in Raub.

The claims of Kuantan to be State capital rested on two essentials – there was unlimited land available for expansion of the town, situated on the narrow coastal plain, and there was no large river in the vicinity, to be a source of flooding with all the dislocation to daily life which sudden floods bring. 'Temporary' government offices had been erected, wooden buildings which accommodated all the State heads of departments, and a hall where the State Council could meet. Thus if any of us acting in a State office wished to consult the head of another department, one did not have to cross a street or drive some distance to the other office, but simply walk a few yards under the 'covered way'. Of course, official accommodation for the officials was at a premium and very scarce, as to be expected in a town which had changed from a district centre to State capital literally overnight.

In our short stay in Pahang we occupied three sets of quarters. On arrival we were given a unit in a 'chalet' similar to that which we had occupied in Kuala Lumpur. Then we had in succession two adjacent houses, where we lived while the respective occupants were on leave.

Pahang produced a most awkward administrative problem, which as will be seen had a tragic sequel, and in my recollection the only really major difficulty in the whole of my service in the Government of Malaya. Shortly before my arrival, a selection board had re-organised the appointments of the head teachers of the English schools, one in each of the six larger towns, all local appointees except for Clifford School, Kuala Lipis, which traditionally had a European principal, that is a member of the Colonial Service. It will be understood that the years after the war had been so concerned with the major tasks of re-establishing the school system and coping with swelling demands for enrolments that minimal attention had been given to staffing and service conditions. As a result of the work of the selection board changes had been made when permanent appointees in some schools replaced the previous acting holders in the positions.

My impression was that the appointments were carefully considered, and the best qualified persons assigned to each post. However, an Indian had been appointed to the school in Pekan, where the sultan resided, taking over from a senior Malay who had some rank and considerable influence, and who was instigating opposition to the headmaster in covert fashion, despite the fact that the sultan had agreed to the new appointment. To summarise events briefly, one night shortly after I had assumed duty the OCPD Pekan rang me to state the police had dragged the body of the unfortunate headmaster from the river, and that the police were treating the case as one of murder. For the next fortnight I travelled down to Pekan and took charge of the school acting as headmaster until I was able to arrange for a new appointment. As may be imagined this was not easy, but I found another Indian who was able to take over the school, the Malay assistant teacher being transferred on the grounds of his attitude. Both the sultan and the teaching body supported my action, to the extent that morale in the schools improved. To my recollection, the police never discovered the perpetrator of the crime.

The school inspection staff consisted of four Malays, two Chinese and one Indian, that being about the respective proportion of the races in Pahang. I had general oversight of all education, with a particular responsibility for the English schools. The small population meant that there were not many qualified young people to become teachers, and all the schools were short of staff, much as those in Johore had been. However, in Kuantan the arrival of the State Headquarters gave an immediate source of employable qualified persons. One woman was a missionary who had been in China with the China Inland Mission, had escaped when the Communists took power in 1949, and now offered her services as a teacher. She had a first-class honours in mathematics from London University, and had taught in

England for several years before becoming a missionary. Such women, and there were many among the wives of government officers and of other Europeans on estates or in commercial concerns, made an enormous contribution to the work of schools. Their value was not confined to the actual classes they taught, but extended to the help and encouragement they gave to the local teachers.

Yvonne Taylor with senior Malay staff of domestic science classes

The fact that Yvonne had worked previously in Malayan schools was known, and suggestions were made that she undertake the duties of State Domestic Science Supervisor, a proposal which had the enthusiastic support of the sultan. The Education Office had a van used to distribute supplies of equipment and stationery, and the driver was made available to conduct Yvonne on her visits to the schools to inspect classes and take courses for the instruction of teachers in the schools. On one occasion I was at home in Kuantan, Yvonne being in the west of the State, when the telephone rang and a police inspector was on the line, with the information that the van had broken down at the village, a few miles from Raub, but he was arranging to take Yvonne to the Rest House for the night. A stop because of accident or breakdown was not a casual matter, and while the Emergency had to a large extent lessened in Pahang, a hold-up by terrorists on the lonely roads through the jungle areas was still a possibility. Enquiry revealed that the breakdown was due, not to faulty maintenance, but to complete neglect of any servicing of the vehicle for months, this detail being forgotten among the changes resulting from the move of the Education Office across the State to Kauntan. Not having had grease application or servicing, the bearings in the wheels had finally seized up. We bought a second car, a used Chevrolet of the model of the previous year. Yvonne got her driving licence, and liked to drive the 'Chev' on her tours of inspection and instruction.

As stated above, Pahang had been one of the Federated Malay States, and despite its difficulties of topography and demography, it showed in various ways the benefit of the longer association with British rule. The main drawback for us in Johore was the absence of any facilities for pre-school education. Kate had a few months at a primary school but Ruth missed out as she was below school age. But in Kuantan the Convent of the Good Samaritan ran a kindergarten, which Mark attended while we lived in the town, and he was able to continue in a school of the same order in Kuala Lumpur. These schools were conducted in the English medium, were managed by European nuns, and were open to children of all races – in itself a useful introduction to life in the modern world.

The climate in Kuantan was markedly milder than that of the western States as there was throughout the year a sea breeze in the evenings, and often during the day as well. We frequently went for a walk along the beach when Mark could go for a paddle; there was no swimming, as the beach extended far towards the water, and even at high tide the water was quite shallow. It was a favourite spot for the owners, of all races, to take their dogs for a run.

The one medical mishap our family sustained in Malaya was in Kuantan, when some months after our arrival a lump appeared in Mark's thigh, which appeared to be persistent. It was diagnosed as an abscess, requiring an operation in hospital. The cause was stated to be the result of the use of a septic needle when Mark was given a penicillin injection in Kuala Kubu by a hospital assistant, while we were in Tanjong Malim. As Mark was only four, the hospital was very keen that Yvonne stay in the ward with him, and the operation proved very successful, with Mark being discharged in a few days.

In Kuantan it was rare for a European child to go to hospital, so Mark was visited unofficially by all the hospital staff who were not concerned with his case as a matter of duty – word got round that 'there is a nice European boy in Ward X'.

We have now reached 1956, the year before Malayan independence. A further story in which Mark played a leading role may indicate the level of development in country districts at this stage. It was suggested by my staff that I should visit a township (Kuala Krai), up the Pahang River north of Temerloh, the centre of the central area of the State. This necessitated arranging to requisition a government launch to take us for the trip. There were two schools in the small town, a Malay and a Chinese, so the respective inspectors in charge of that area came with me, as did Yvonne and Mark for a day's outing. The reason for the visit was some difficulty with the state of the buildings and of school staffing. I was told that I was the first chief education officer to make the trip. Under the guidance of the inspectors I made my way to each school in turn, met the teachers and viewed the problems which needed attention. Yvonne and Mark followed us up the main street (perhaps the only street) and looking back I saw they were followed by apparently the whole population, men and women, at a respectful distance, with the cry 'Mari sini, tengok mem dangan anak' ('Come quickly, look at the European lady and her child'). Yvonne was probably the only European woman, and Mark certainly the only European child, these people had ever seen. Needless to say, the visit was quite a success in many ways. They had had other visits by European officers, a district officer certainly, and perhaps a PWD engineer, but even these only on rare occasions.

The following description will describe the capital difficulty of administration in a State such as Pahang. Admittedly it was the largest, and with more and different problems than the others. Most of the schools were small, in villages or small townships, of populations of a few hundred each, but there would have been at least two hundred of them in all – English, Malay, Chinese and Indian. My visit to the two schools described would take all of one working day – rising at dawn, about 6 a.m., to cover the distance by car from Kuantan to Temerloh, 100 miles, well over two hours' travelling; an hour by launch each way to the township, and an hour inspecting the schools, with finally the return drive to Kauntan, which we reached after offices had closed for the day. For myself and the two inspectors all our other duties were simply left in abeyance during our absence. Most of the population, especially the Malays, lived in villages along the Pahang River and its tributaries, which indeed defined the area of the State, the rivers having their sources in the central mountain chain, and flowing east. In addition there were some tin mines and rubber estates, under European or Chinese ownership, and with labour forces mainly Chinese and Indian respectively. A railway ran from the south in an adjoining State, roughly up the centre of Pahang, finally passing through the northern State of Kelantan to its capital on the east coast. There were small towns on the railway, which were not accessible by river or road. The settlements along the roads were usually remote from the rivers and the railways. Thus the localities within easy reach of transport were those on the roads. In practical terms, it was not possible to visit places on the railway at all, owing to the inconvenient timetables – night travel made visits during office hours impossible.

Villages situated on the rivers could be visited by water craft. For government officers this consisted of 'house boats', a barge with sleeping and eating facilities, towed by a motor launch. The arranging of a river tour of inspection was itself a major operation; there were from memory at most two house boats, and district officers, particularly, would need to visit their areas at regular intervals. Thus an application to use the transport had to be made months in advance; the usual trip being up river at Jarantut, at which town the road met the Pahang River where there was a vehicle ferry, then proceeded down the river to its estuary at Pekan, where the sultan resided. The distance from Kauntan to Jerantut was over 100 miles, over three hours by car; the officials boarded the house boat on Saturday evening,[17] in time to berth alongside the first village to be inspected next day. In the five days of the week a daily average of three schools, which were about evenly divided on each bank of the river, were visited, allowing about an hour at each school, and travelling time of an hour between schools, which worked for five hours from before 8 a.m. to 1 p.m. The afternoon would be spent in travelling down to the next village to be visited next day.

My river tour occurred about 12 months after my arrival in Pahang in November, and of course I knew I was risking running into the monsoon season. The Saturday on which I embarked was a lovely sunny day, and so was the next day, but the day following it began to rain in the afternoon, not heavily, but increasing in intensity during the days that followed. The rainfall at the point of the river where I happened to be was obviously not important; what did matter was the deluge taking place in the mountain ranges where the tributaries had their sources. As rain falls fairly evenly throughout the year, the river was never lower than a few feet below the top of its banks, and continuous rain in the monsoon could have only one result – flooding. Each morning the boatman brought me my breakfast, and in response to my enquiry about the river level his reply was the same each day, 'Six inches higher, sir.' There was nothing I could do but continue with the tour day by day as planned. All the schools on the river received a visit; my umbrella was used on several occasions, but no long walks were necessary, as the villages were close to the river bank; all, that is, except for the last two schools on the outskirts of Pekan, where the river was already lapping over the banks, covering the schools' grounds with water, making it necessary to close the schools. As this was one of the former Federated Malay States the official week followed western practice, extending from Monday to Friday, not as in the other States, such as Jahore, from Sunday to Thursday. A Malay inspector was waiting for me, as arranged, at Pekan and drove me home the 28 miles to Kuantan. As luck would have it, that was the only week of monsoon weather that year. I was therefore able to work in the office on Friday and Saturday morning.

As mentioned above, our daughters started school in Perth in 1955, and each year we had them home for two months, from early December to early February, during the long southern summer vacation. Most days we were able to take the girls for an evening picnic to Beserah six miles north of Kuantan where swimming was available. Offices closed at 4.30 p.m., so it was possible to have an hour on the beach and return at dusk, which varied during the year about half an hour from 6 p.m.; remembering that at this latitude, about 3° N, the sun is overhead twice each 12 months.

An important social occasion was the regular reception given by the sultan in Pekan every few months, held in the palace or 'Istana'. We drove down to the river, were taken over to the town by launch and returned later. There was of course a traditional protocol at these gatherings, but the sultan was informal in manner, a big man physically and an intelligent and energetic ruler. He spent much of his time visiting the villages, even the most remote, and on these visits he would often invite European officers of various departments to join his party, to assist in dealing with problems encountered by the people. However, the sultan contented himself with conversation with us at these social gatherings, as he evidently thought that Yvonne and I did enough visiting in Malay villages in the course of our work. It was a normal matter of protocol for guests to leave only after a formal leave from the sultan at the end of the proceedings. However, the sultan agreed to permit us to leave earlier, on the grounds that we had to get up early the next morning to begin our travelling. Needless to say, this 'gracious permission' never failed to impress the gathering, made up as it always was of people of all races.

One further example of the sultan's informality – he once came to visit me in my office with the request, as did most of my callers, that I could advise on education for his two sons reaching secondary school age. There was an English school at Kuala Lipis, the former capital where there was a school hostel for boys. The headmaster, a European, was able to accommodate the two lads – the sultan's view was that he wanted to have the boys close enough to 'keep his eye on them', instead of sending them away to the Malay college or to a school overseas, which had been a common practice for the Malay sultans for very many years under British rule. The sultan visited Australia while we lived in Perth and did us the honour of inviting us to his hotel for an evening when we talked of old times.

One episode during my visits to Malay schools caused some amusement among the staff in the department. It was my practice to leave home early enough to arrive at the first school on my itinerary at about the official time of opening. The school was situated about 40 miles west from Kuantan on the main road, at a picturesque spot where there was a succession of small lakes alongside the road. I had been some months in Pahang, but as the villages were widely scattered few people outside the towns recognised my car, distinctive as a steel-grey Austin A90. I pulled up alongside the road by the school, where the grounds were right by the road. Instead of finding the pupils lined up in the grounds, assembled to enter school – the usual practice – there was no sign that lessons were to begin for some time; children were slowly making their way along the road to school, others playing unconcernedly in the playground, when I opened the car door, took my bag, and began to make my way to the school building. It is safe to say that never in any school in Malaya was action more sudden, unpremeditated, or with such rapid and comprehensive results. The head teacher was shaving in the top floor of his house adjacent to the school, saw me, and dashed out of the house, calling to a boy to ring the school bell. His assistant teacher, enjoying a quiet cup of coffee in the coffee shop opposite the school, heard the bell, left his coffee and dashed across the road. The effect on the pupils was electric; at the sound of the bell, games in progress dissolved and the participants dashed into line; those sauntering in leisurely fashion on the road sprang into action and raced towards the school, while those more distant saw there was some crisis, and appeared out of houses or from jungle paths onto the road, as if by magic.

That, indeed, was the end of the story; there was no need for me to say a word. The wretched (no other word can describe him) head teacher was 'in shock' and suitably contrite. I asked to see some of the children's work, which was generally untidy and careless, as could be expected. With a promise to return in a few weeks, I took my departure from the dazed two teachers and fifty or so pupils.

This episode illustrates the geographical conditions in the State. The narrow riverine strips along the river banks were fertile, and the villages correspondingly prosperous, the people well fed and active. In the eastern district the land was poor, and the people made a precarious livelihood from fishing. Their physical and mental development and well-being were markedly inferior to that of people in the western districts and in the river districts. Ulu Luit (the village concerned in the incident), though on the main road, was quite isolated, and many miles on either side from the next village. I doubt whether there would have been any settlement at all, but for the lakes, which would supply fish, and the streams feeding the lakes, which made some cultivation possible. I did visit the school again some time later; the improvements were such as to make the school almost unrecognisable, due to the special attention given by the Malay inspector of the district.

An important experience that Pahang gave us was the sighting of 'our' tiger. The horrific tales of the depredations made by these lovely animals were in fact based on rare occurrences, and arose, we were told, only when an old animal was no longer active enough to catch its normal prey in the jungle. The encounter happened one night when we were driving home from attending one of the sultan's receptions in Pekan. The road runs near to the coast and was really a succession of straight stretches connected by easy curves. As the coastal strip was swampy and low-lying, the road for much of the way ran along a raised embankment with deep drains on either side. Rounding a bend, we saw some distance ahead a frisky animal, cream-buff in colour, in size similar to a Jersey heifer, a common sight on New Zealand roads. We slowed down, and as we approached we saw that its coat was actually marked with stripes, as it gambolled from side to side on the road. After we stopped, some yards away from the animal, the glare of the headlights seemed to dazzle its eyes and it turned round, glanced at us, and shot into the bushes beside the road. Two young forestry officers lived near us, and left in our keeping their MG while they did their jungle tours. They told us that to sight a tiger even in the jungle is quite rare, and indeed forestry officials could leave the country after many years of duty in jungle exploration without sighting this national symbol of Malaya.

As will have become apparent, my time in Pahang was largely spent in devising means of ensuring effective administration and guidance for education in the State. Owing to the distances involved, it seemed that the time was most economically used by touring for a whole week, at intervals of a month or so. The week visiting schools on the Pahang River has been described. The only direct road connecting Kuala Lumpur with Kuantan had been by way of a road branching off the main north–south highway at Kuala Kubu, in north Selangor, then passing over the central range near the Fraser's Hill Holiday Station (where the High Commissioner was assassinated in 1951), then winding through jungle covered valleys in the north of Pahang, passing through Raub, the only town of any size on the route.

The Pahang River was crossed by ferry at Jerantut. But shortly before my arrival a new road, contributed by the British Colonial Development Agency, branched through the jungle south from the old road at Maran, about 50 miles from Kuantan, until it met the Pahang River at Termeloh, the centre of the central district. Thus was formed a rough oblong, on which was situated three of the chief towns; Kuala Lipis was connected by a branch road of 16 miles at the northern point of the oblong; so it was possible to visit these towns, and a number of smaller ones on a circuit, with only the branch road to Kuala Lipis and the Kuantan-Maran stretch having to be covered in return trips. It was a total distance of over 350 miles, much of it on narrow winding roads. At the end of each day I stayed at the local Rest House where I held 'open house' to all who wished to see me, an invaluable means of getting acquainted with the teachers and their problems, and with the physical conditions under which they worked.

Naturally the work of the office went on as usual in my absence, and on my return my first task was to deal with the piles of office files awaiting my attention and decision. On one occasion these files were piled so high on the trolley between my table and the office window that I was obscured from passers-by on the covered way outside the office. Of course, after my long absence, a number of officers in other departments wished to discuss matters with me. Not seeing me, they asked the chief clerk, who assured callers that I was indeed working in the office. Finally, one official came in the door and looked round the barrier made by the file trolley, and saw that indeed the boss was back at work. Saturday morning was a half-day in government offices, and by the end of the session I had cleared these matters only requiring a signature or a minute, leaving the problems for my consideration outside office hours, and allowing my head to be visible again to those glancing through the window.

The end of my term in Pahang came suddenly and unexpectedly, but to understand the circumstances a brief outline of the constitutional position is necessary. The first elections for any legislative body in Malaya were held in mid-1955, for the Federal Legislative Council, held while I was at Tanjong Malim, as noted above. The usual system in British Colonial Territories was to have a legislative council where members were either senior government officials, or prominent local citizens appointed by the government. These councils had considerable powers of passing and amending legislation, and though ultimately the governor had overriding powers, in practice, these were rarely invoked, as the aim of any government must be to act in accordance with popular opinion, or at least not in opposition to it.

A Constitutional Commission, composed of leading jurists from several Commonwealth countries including Britain, Canada, India and Australia, spent several months in the country in 1956, drawing up a draft Constitution for Independent Malaya. I was interviewed by the Commission on its visit to Kuantan. Following this, a delegation of senior members of the elected federal government went to London, and negotiated with British Government officials a 'Federation of Malaya Agreement', which was in fact an independence treaty. In due course this was ratified in London and in Kuala Lumpur. For serving European (British) officers the main provision was that we were to leave on early retirement, the latest dates for which were fixed varying in accordance with the government department of each officer; in the Education Department the date was 1962. Officers could retire at any time after 1 July 1957, all officers still in employment on that date being eligible for the special terms of retirement. In brief, in addition to the pension accrued in the usual way of service, a lump sum gratuity was granted, graduated according to the perceived hardship incurred by loss of career. This was arranged to give a maximum grant at the age of 39, when officers had gained experience and could normally expect to fill senior posts later in their careers, but the grant declined little for officers in their early forties: the grant for new arrivals at one end, and those near the normal retiring age of 55, was minimal.

From 1956 elections were held State by State on the same lines as for the Federation Legislative Council, the Pahang Council being elected by early 1957. As chief education officer I was a member of council as an official, and continued as such when the appointed unofficial members were replaced by elected members for the various electoral districts.

It was accordingly quite clear that, though we had a breathing space of a few years, the 'expatriate' officers, as those appointed from Britain were called, had now as their main preoccupation the planning of their immediate future and that of their families, and many officers, especially the older ones, immediately sent in their application to retire on or about 1 July 1957.

The elected council in Pahang had met once or twice, without any apparent major difficulty arising, the main difference being the many questions asked by the elected members, few of which concerned the schools, most being concerned with such matters as roads, agricultural concerns of the villages, or health services. At the next meeting, about March 1957, I noticed that the atmosphere was not at all friendly, and I was not surprised to learn that the government party caucus[18] which was mainly Malay, but supported by Chinese and Indians, was going to move a vote of no confidence against the Education Department.

This United Party, composed of the parties representing each racial group, the combination being known as the Alliance, had practically won every seat in every State council, except in Kelantan. At this date I cannot even remember what the complaint was, although in view of the rapid post-war expansion of the schools, deficiencies of one kind and another were not hard to find; one of our problems was that the schools hastily erected after the war had succumbed to white ants, and it was quite common for teachers and pupils to return after a weekend to find their schoolroom had collapsed. This problem, more severe in Pahang in our difficult environment, was only just being surmounted by the use of specially treated timber which, though not of course permanent, would last for a number of years in that wet and humid climate. My memory is that the motion was not put to the vote; the president of council was the chief minister, who supported me in saying simply that complaints would be investigated.

The news of the action of the caucus had considerable repercussions. The sultan was furious, and I believe expressed his displeasure most forcibly to those concerned, and the effect on the Education Department staff was one of anger and disbelief. Of course, the motion of the caucus was in effect interpreted as a notice that they would not cooperate with the working of the State Education Department while I was in office. It so happened that the chief education officer, Selangor, a pre-war appointee who had survived the infamous Siam railway, wanted to retire immediately, so I was telephoned by the director of education asking me to take over the Selangor State Education Department which I did immediately. My predecessor's family had already gone overseas, so we were able to move into the residence straight away.

On balance, the Pahang caucus had done nobody any real harm, except themselves. I do not remember that any similar action was taken in any other council in the next three years while we lived in Malaya. And I gathered that my appointment in Selangor was regarded as fortunate, as I already knew the State well from my residence in Klang earlier in my career. For Yvonne and me, it was a move to be among old friends, and our last term in the country proved both useful and enjoyable. It was quite obvious that the attitude of the Prime Minister and government was that the expatriate officers were to be courteously treated if they continued to serve after independence. If we had all gone at the date of independence, severe confusion would have resulted. Perhaps it is unnecessary to add that my European successor and the staffs of the Education Office continued to carry on my reforms without any variation or changes in policy or methods.

With regard to Pahang, perhaps two further incidents will illustrate aspects of the conditions attendant on working in this State. The sudden action of the Alliance caucus did not come as a complete surprise. As will be evident from the account, an unpleasant undertone had the apparent intention of causing the maximum effect of a 'surprise attack'.

Knowledge of the previous history of the State was sufficient warning that anything could happen.[19] Understandably, a posting to Pahang was the least attractive assignment to government officials, not only for Europeans, but possibly more so for local people. Difficulties in staffing the Pahang English schools has been described; it was very difficult to attract any government officials, teachers or others, to accept a position in Pahang, even on promotion. Just before my move to Pahang, I was visiting the Federal Education Office and the deputy director asked me 'Well, Taylor, how do you like the idea of going to "darkest Pahang"?'

The first such incident occurred on one of my 'round tours' of the State and stopping at Temerloh I was told to attend a meeting at the English school. There I found Datu Abdul Razak, the Federal Member for Temerloh, later Deputy Prime Minister, with a small gathering, all looking unhappy. At the time, the Federal Education Department was making a general statistical survey of the schools, which entailed individual returns from the schools. The notice of the survey came out during the Fasting Month, when Muslims do not eat during the day, and the Malay schools were always closed on holiday for this month. The survey was proceeding with the other schools, but the Malay inspectors suggested to me that we postpone the survey till the Malay schools reopened, and they assured me that they would complete the survey by the date required by Kuala Lumpur.

Apparently the complaint at the meeting was that the Malay schools were being left out of the survey, and the accusation was inferred that I was 'discriminating against' the Malays, a really serious political offence. My explanation was grudgingly accepted, and I inferred that some at least of the newly elected council members were taking no time in raising complaints.

The second incident, about the same time, perhaps on the same tour, allows me to end on a happier note. As the schools in Malaya were open from about 8 a.m. to 1 p.m., of course any visits had to be made during these times. Thus the time was filled by necessarily short visits and travelling between schools. I kept with me a Thermos flask of coffee, so was able to stop anywhere on the roadside for a drink when convenient. On this occasion, I happened to stop on the road outside a Malay girls' school which was not on my list of visits. Sadly, on inspecting tours my visits were restricted to the problems to which I was referred by my inspectors. I had just poured my mug of coffee, when out of the school ran the Malay headmistress, calling out 'Tabek, tuan; suka memereksa sekolahah saya?' ('Greetings, Sir, would you like to inspect my school?'). As one would expect, the whole place was a delight in every way: relationships between the teachers and girls excellent, and the general standard of work in keeping. So the few minutes of my stay were a pleasant interlude for me and for the teachers and pupils. As has been mentioned in this account, a great source of satisfaction in my work in Pahang was to see excellent work evident in schools of every type, achieved usually despite quite severe handicaps. And that is the abiding memory which Yvonne and I have of our time in this State.

Chapter 7
Selangor, 1957–1960

The date for Malayan independence had been set for August 1957, and one provision of the agreement between the British and Malayan Governments was to allow any British official to retire on full pension, and if the date of leaving the service was after 1 July 1957, to qualify for compensation for loss of career, on a sliding scale, those most severely disadvantaged being officers aged 39. As accrued leave could be counted towards meeting the cut-off date, by the time I arrived in April about a third of the entitled officers had retired, or had applied to do so. The main problem for the government in the years immediately following independence was to retain enough of the senior officers to ensure a smooth transition to the time when the Government Service was fully staffed by local personnel. Without the intervention of the Pahang Alliance caucus it is therefore probable that I might have been transferred to Selangor anyway.

Tree planting at a country high school 1958; headmaster on right

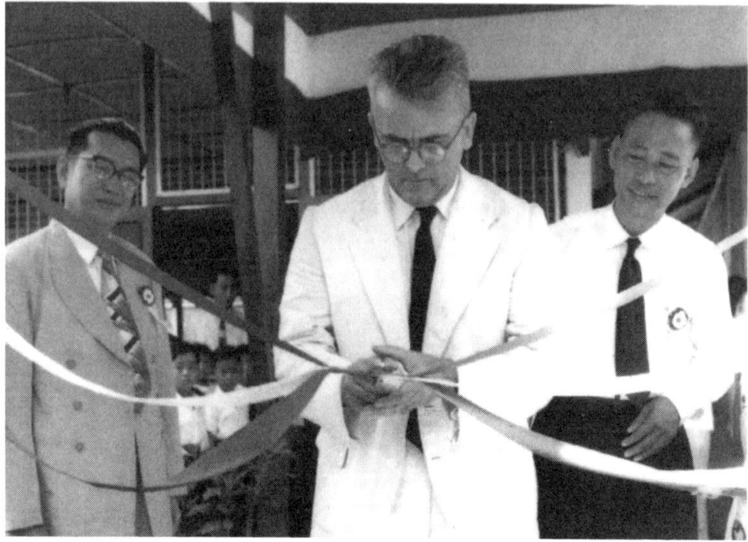

Opening a new Chinese school, Kuala Lumpur 1958

Selangor, then with a population of a million, over three times that of Pahang, was second only to Perak, which had about a million and a quarter people. As will have been learnt earlier in this account, my service in Malaya was generally attended by good fortune, few problems of really major difficulty having occurred. If possible, our last three years were still more free of official misadventure, with the added bonus that we were among the friends whom we had made during our stay in Klang, which had finished less than seven years before. Most of the principals of the aided English schools were the same as I had known while I was at Klang, and the staff of the State Education Office had been stable for a number of years – not a common feature in most offices of post-war Malaya. The sultan had his principal residence in Klāng, and was the one with whom we had had frequent acquaintance while residing in the town. As the position was vacant, Yvonne was asked to undertake the duties of domestic science supervisor, and accordingly was associated with many of the teachers whom she had trained while working in Klang.

Selangor was small in area, smaller than any State except tiny Perlis in the north and the settlements of Penang and Malacca. It was therefore easy to visit any school in any part of the State and return to my headquarters in Kuala Lumpur in one day, except for Sabah Bernam, to the north on the coast where a stay overnight was necessary. Obviously, the difference this made to administration was enormous, a complete contrast to the work in Pahang, where information was normally received through the staff inspectors or by correspondence, either procedure being subject to some long delay if some protracted investigation or a lengthy report was necessary. Whenever the situation so warranted it, in Selangor I was able in a few hours to visit a school, consult with all those concerned – the head teacher, the inspector of schools, local people, the district officer or PWD engineer – and decide on a programme of action. Then followed the necessary work by those involved, who had the advantage of attending the conference where the views of the other participants had been heard. An important effect of this expeditious handling of building and other major items was the increased morale of everyone – the teachers, the village people, and the office staff, who could see projects taking shape soon after they were approved.

The main problem with education in Selangor was the effort to keep up with the demand of enrolments, especially in Kuala Lumpur and its suburbs. The largest suburb was Petaling Jaya, a new satellite suburb which had been established a few years before, and was adding to its population as fast as building sections could be surveyed and sold and homes erected. Kuala Lumpur, for the first time in its history, was experiencing the problems of a national metropolis. Pre-war it was merely the administrative centre for the four Federated Malay States and for the State of Selangor. After the Federation of Malaya came into existence in February 1948, it became the federal capital for nine States and two Settlements, all of which were in a uniform constitutional relationship with the federal government and with each other. In Asian countries, the concentration of power in one town as capital has a more rapid effect on the increase of population than elsewhere – Jakarta, Bangkok and Seoul are mong the world's largest cities, and Kuala Lumpur was beginning the rapid growth which has continued ever since.

Preparations for the independence celebrations were well advanced when I arrived. A stadium which seated over 20,000 people had been built in anticipation, and there the main events of the week's celebrations were held. These included the actual independence ceremony which marked the official end of British rule, in which HRH the Duke of Gloucester officiated as representative of the Queen. Later in the same day there were ceremonies in Malacca and Penang, which had been actual British colonies, in contrast to the Malay States, which were protected states under conditions of various treaties. The Education Department had organised a physical education demonstration by 4,000 pupils from various schools.

There was also a military tattoo, and receptions by the Prime Minister, who changed his title from Chief Minister on the day of independence. At the conclusion of that day, the High Commissioner took his leave of leading political figures, community leaders and government officers, including especially the British officials who had served in his (Sir Donald McGillivray's) term and that of his predecessor, Sir Gerald Templer, who himself was a guest of the government during the celebrations. Our residence adjoined that of the Prime Minister, and on his way to a reception Sir Gerald called on us unexpectedly, got out of his car and asked to park it on our drive until he returned. I had never met him while he was High Commissioner; he greeted Yvonne and me in his usual cordial and informal manner, at one point putting his field-marshal's hat on the head of our son Mark, then 6 years old. Mark had cemented a friendship with the police and military guards on duty at the gate of the Prime Minister's residences adjoining our entrance. It was a general custom for the governor in British Territories overseas to give a reception on the sovereign's birthday, which was then celebrated in June. We were therefore resident in Kuala Lumpur in time to attend the last Queen's birthday observance in Kuala Lumpur while it was under British rule.

An attempt was made to provide for community involvement in education by having Education Boards in each State, instead of the control by a chief education officer, who worked in association with the State government, in consultation with the Chief Minister. Though the States were in control of the running of their Education Departments, the education budget was approved by the Federal Legislative Council and most of the finance came from the federal government, which controlled salary scales and conditions of service, curricula, school regulations, and standards of buildings and equipment. The general effect of this system was to make for uniform standards among the various States and bring the conditions of the former Unfederated States into line with the more advanced Settlements and Federated States. Of course, in the 11 years since the war the process of standardisation had not proceeded very far or uniformly, and at the time of independence there were wide variations in the facilities available from one State to another.

The building of new schools and extensions to existing schools was the main preoccupation during my term of office. My chief concern was to obtain school sites, not an easy task for two reasons – land was in short supply in the towns, as the population was already dense in many areas; and in that very wet climate, much of the land was waterlogged or subject to flooding, and therefore the

With the Sultan of Selangor at school sports 1958

preparation of the foundations of buildings in low-lying or swampy localities was often as expensive as the cost of the actual building. These problems involved discussions with the PWD engineers and the finance authorities, which formed the most time-consuming part of my work.

Some devolution of responsibility occurred when the Kuala Lumpur municipality formed its own Education Department to run the primary schools, but secondary schools remained under State control. I was pleased to be able to devote more attention to the rural schools, which in the nature of prevailing circumstances were over-shadowed by the incessant demands for accommodation by the swelling numbers in the towns. Developments at the port city of Klang were almost as rapid as those in the capital.

A feature of Malayan life that continued throughout our stay in the country was the good social attitude which existed between the communities despite the background of the Emergency, along with a readiness to appreciate humorous incidents. One of the schools which extended its buildings in my term was the Methodist Girls’

School in Klang where Yvonne had taught while we lived in Klang. Yvonne and I had been invited to the opening ceremony and I was directed to the official platform, while Yvonne sat in the front row of the audience, with the heads of the local schools and community leaders. The Methodists administered their schools through an Education Office, presided over by an education secretary. This official had changed during the construction of the buildings, and we had not met previously. During his address to the gathering he introduced me as 'the new chief education officer' (which I was) and went on to say that 'though I was a stranger to them they looked forward to my better acquaintance'. Yvonne and I never forgot the look of sheer amazement registered on every face – Yvonne the reaction of those on the platform, while I shared the surprise evident among the audience. The incident provided a light relief for the proceedings, and resulted in good humour all round, including the education secretary, who was unlucky in the occasion for his comments.

A polio epidemic was the most important difficulty which arose, having severe implications for the health of the young people. A number of cases were reported throughout the Peninsula and in Singapore, and of course there was popular demand that the schools should be closed. The government had introduced inoculations with the Salk vaccine in 1951, and this epidemic, about seven years later, was the last severe polio epidemic to occur. The State medical health officer (a Malay) had been medical officer of health in Klang when we worked in that town, and we devised a common plan of campaign, the main point being that the schools would remain open as usual. Polio is infectious, so the main means of reducing this incidence is to eliminate close public contact. In local conditions, the children were in better circumstances in the schools than they were in their small and overcrowded homes or while playing in the narrow streets or attending cinema shows. We put out joint public notices in the media, in consultation with the Chief Minister, and our incidence of cases compared favourably with other States and with Singapore, some of whom resorted to closing the schools.

We went on leave in December 1957 and called at Perth to attend the end-of-year function at the girls' school, and then accompanied them to New Zealand for the summer holidays. The girls returned to school early in February.

I returned in April to duty in Kuala Lumpur, and Yvonne in May, after visiting Malayan friends who had retired in Perth, where we thought we should make our retirement home. The girls spent their summer holidays with us in Kuala Lumpur the next two years, and we thus had them at home each summer while they were boarding at school. This was a very valuable arrangement, as we were enabled to stay in contact with them and they with us, until we left the country, and thus mitigate the period of separation of children from their parents, which was a difficult feature of European life in the tropics.

Our life and work continued as happily as before, and followed the annual round of duties incidental to the administration of an education system. In practice this meant working a year ahead of the functioning of the schools. The planning of next year's budget began as soon as the schools had settled down for the year in January. All sections of the office submitted proposals for school buildings, staffing, training of teachers and acquisition of equipment, which required incorporation on the official forms and consultation with other councils. These included the PWD, who had to oversee the buildings and land offices for requisition of land for sites, for each of which we were dependent on the cooperation and goodwill of those offices. As stated above, quite often it was expedient to visit offices in the various districts for consultation which, though time consuming, in the end made for increased expedition in completing projects.

But most of the European officers then had as their main concern their own future and that of their families, those of us in mid-career requiring to obtain employment wherever we decided to settle. By staying for a period after independence we increased the amount of pension which we could anticipate to receive, but all the time we as parents, and also our children, were growing older as important years slipped by. The inauguration of elected State councils proceeded in succession, one at a time, and the process was enacted in Selangor later in the sequence during my term of office. The main effect on our office work was the addition of queries and requests from the elected members, who were eager to impress their constituents; of course the extra work was a time consuming burden to the office staff.

It will be clear that in our last years among our official duties the preparation for independence had priority, and to be able to do our part it was essential that we (the chief education officers of the States) should receive full and accurate briefing on the changes proposed. In no department of government were the changes more radical than in education. The first innovation was to make Malay a compulsory subject in every school. Previously the non-Malay schools had included Malay only as an optional subject, and in fact the Chinese and Tamil schools had taught English more often than Malay. The ultimate intention of making Malay the medium of instruction in all schools was also announced.

A further departure from previous practice was to make the senior post in the Federal Education Department a position for an administrative officer, instead of a professional education officer. The administration of education is a problem in every country, because promoting teachers to administrative posts means that those teachers, usually the best, are taken out of the classroom and placed behind an office table. On the other hand, it is essential for the administrator to know what goes on, and 'have a feel for' conditions in a school in arranging for school staffing, as well as in approving building plans, and in many other matters. The change in the head office administration was made just before independence, and there were indications of the adoption of a routine and mechanical procedure, in contrast to the aim of fitting new systems into the particular places where they were expected to operate, after consultation where desirable. As will be noted later, Yvonne and I were to experience the working of the new system before we left the country.

For the record, as a family we were fortunate in our health during our time in the country. Mark, as stated above, had an operation for an abscess in his thigh resulting from an infected needle; Yvonne had three months in hospital with a digestive complaint caused by sampling tainted food in a school cooking lesson, while my misfortune was limited to a few days with dysentery caused by food at the Prime Minister's Independence Reception. As is to be expected, disorders of the digestive system were the most common health problems of European residents in the country. This was despite the high standard of medical and health services established during this century. In our time in Kuala Lumpur it was unnecessary to sleep under mosquito nets; reports of malaria cases were very rare, even in remote country areas.

Following these considerations, I applied for retirement on 'Malayanisation' at the end of 1959, and we left the Service in February 1960. We received farewells by each of the different sections of the schools, and the domestic science teachers gave Yvonne a special parting function. Mark accompanied his sisters to a boarding school when they returned in February. I had accumulated eight months' leave, which enabled us to arrange to purchase a house, and also to leave the children at their boarding schools for the rest of the year, the intention being that they could attend the same schools as day pupils the following year. We were fortunate once more that the plans came to fruition, and the children had the minimum difficulty in the transition to residence in a temperate country; all three had, of course, been born in the tropics, and had spent their early childhood years in that environment.

Primary school sports, Kuala Lumpur 1959; Yvonne Taylor presenting prizes

This seems a suitable point at which to express our valedictory comments on our time of service in the country. First, we should wish to record our abiding impression of the friendliness of the people, all races and all classes of society, from the sultans to the labourers in field and factory; from our first days in the country until we left on retirement, it was indeed the 'Land of Smiles'. I have described my first morning at King Edward VII School Taiping. A few days later the British Resident, the senior government official in the State, visited the school apparently on a brief informal visit, his first after the resumption of British rule after the Japanese occupation. The school staff were asked to assemble during the school interval to meet the Resident, Mr J. Ashton, who retired from the Service soon afterwards. He glanced round the gathering, came right across the hall where we were all standing, said he had not met me, and greeted me, as the principal explained I was the 'new arrival' from New Zealand. Of course, I never forgot this welcome, and it confirmed the impression of an immediate and warm introduction to the country and to the Service, after which it was impossible to feel a stranger.

Over the years I retain memories of risings at dawn, and driving along the roads, perhaps still partially blanketed in mist, passing groups of rubber tappers, market gardeners, numerous persons riding bicycles all going to the places of their daily work. And

Selangor Education Office staff 1959

always, at a village school, or large city secondary school, being assured of a smiling welcome, looked upon as a friend, rather than just as an official, subject to the call of duty.

All the communities shared each others' festivals – we received Christmas cards and in turn sent cards and were invited to the gatherings for and the End of Fasting Month (Malay and Indian Muslims), Chinese New Year, and Deepavali (Hindu). Both official and private occasions were colourful and impressive, the women especially attractive, decked out in their delightful national costumes.

Our working days were made the more productive by the friendly attitude of all concerned – from the senior officials, Europeans and locals, to the clerk and message boys ('peons'). The few occasions when different situations arose, remarkably few in retrospect, have been noted in passing as they occurred. It is thus my view, that the conditions we experienced were the result of the work of our predecessors, the generations of British officials and of the local people who developed the country to the level of achievement, with which we grew familiar. We remained grateful and appreciative of all the kindness and assistance which was bestowed on us during those years.

The Malayan experience: conclusion

It is now over 40 years since I retired from the Malayan Government Service, and almost that interval of years since the Colonial Office was finally closed (1966), signifying the conclusion of the existence of the British Empire in its last remaining section – the other two parts, the Indian Empire and the Dominions, having gained independent status during the previous 50 years or so. The first question is clearly a personal one – was the experience of 14 years worthwhile? My answer is clearly 'Yes'. My main interest has always been the history and development of countries, of any country, that of my birth or of any other. However, the 'Far East' is in fact the nearest continent to Australia and New Zealand, and it is clear will have a permanent influence on the future of both the latter countries. My Malayan experience is invaluable in enabling me to understand the way Asians work and think, reinforced by considerable study of their historical and geographical background.

Clearly my own education and upbringing in New Zealand was different in many ways from that of my British colleagues, varied as they were among themselves in their origins – every university in the British Isles was represented by members of the staff, including Trinity College, Dublin, and the University of Wales. My degree in Classics and English, followed by a Diploma in Education were on paper similar to those of my associates. The main difference was in the amount of specialisation; the British people usually taught in secondary schools for a few years in their subject before going overseas, while in the smaller school system of New Zealand, whose population is less than several English shires, some teaching in primary schools is usually a necessary part of a teaching career. This feature was a considerable asset when I came to administer schools at a State level, as in any complete educational system primary (or elementary) schools outnumber secondary schools in enrolments as well as in the number of separate institutions. The primary supervisors, who actually did most of the inspecting and advising in the schools, could tell the teachers that the 'boss' had taught in primary schools himself, which intelligence had a salutary effect in the work of the schools, and of course in my relationship with the staffs.

Entering the Service as an 'outsider' from 'down under', I formed an objective, and favourable view of the work of the British administrations up to the time of my arrival. As indicated above, the realisation of the value of western education among the local races came very slowly, and that mainly among the wealthier Chinese, Eurasian and Indian communities, who sent a steady trickle of able students overseas, mainly to Britain, from the last quarter of the nineteenth century. These gifted people returned to the Straits Settlements (Singapore, Malacca and Penang), and by the middle of the century there was a small but highly capable, local middle class comprising professional people, officials in government administration and leaders in commercial life – remembering that when the Second World War broke out, Singapore had for many years been one of the top dozen or so international ports in the world. However, progress was not reached even at this level in the Malay States, and I was told by headmistresses in some Perak girls' schools, how they knocked on the doors of leading members of Chinese and Indian families coaxing parents to send their daughters to schools as late as the 1920s. The attitude of the Malays changed still more slowly, and the Malay Girls' College, for daughters of the sultans and Malay aristocracy, was not due to open until 1942; it finally commenced in 1946, after the war.

In addition to the increasing demands for independence among the colonial peoples, the British Empire had little support on the international scene, the two super powers, the USA and the USSR, being the principal opponents, the foreign policy of each having as a main aim the dismantling of the Colonial Empires of Britain, France, the Netherlands and Portugal. An interesting sidelight of this aspect of history is that the United States only in 1992 gave up its last military base in the Philippines; the Soviet Empire only ceased control of its congeries of states, many of them in Asia, when the system itself collapsed as a result of the political change in the last two years, especially the fall of the Berlin Wall in 1989.

In general, it appears that most comment and assessment of the Colonial Empire in recent years has been unfavourable, often antagonistic to such an extent that the words 'colonial' and 'colonialism' have been used as terms of abuse in the international political debate. During my period of service in Malaya government officials were kept informed on this topic, overseas as well as in Malaya. The local press was well in touch with the former, and, as far as British colonies were concerned, developments in the colonies, especially anything which might serve as a cause for criticism, were liable to be taken up in the British Parliament. In Malaya itself, the government issued a weekly abstract of all unfavourable comment appearing in the local press in all the languages, in an English translation. Of course, any important matter was referred to the office concerned for report or action as necessary, but it was understood that information from any officer who had special knowledge of the situation would be welcomed by the administration.

There was therefore a continuous opportunity to assess the efficiency, not only of one's own department, but of the total effect of government functions as well. Occasionally a serious lapse, or a default of necessary action, was reported, but from the standpoint of those in charge of government operations, the problems were usually due to lack of finance, lack of staff, or simply to the greater priority of concerns considered more important.

My only further comment concerns the rate of progress towards the achievement of independence. I arrived in Malaya in June 1946 and attended the independence celebrations in August 1957, just a little over 11 years later. At the beginning of this period the country was severely damaged, socially and materially, by the effects of the Japanese occupation, and at least the basic essentials had to be made good before any advances in administration, transport and communication, or social services, were possible. Overriding all these endeavours was the requirement to overcome the communist insurrection on which all else clearly depended.

Added to the problems of a country that had been under enemy occupation was a severe worldwide post-war shortage of every economic resource – 'men, materials and money'. Much of Europe was even more ravaged by war than was Malaya, and for many years these countries were mainly engaged in rebuilding their economies, with the important assistance of the United States by its 'Marshall Plan'. Britain had suffered greatly from war-time bombing, and for several years after the war food was in short supply, so that the Commonwealth countries, Australia, New Zealand and Canada, were asked to augment the food supply as much as possible. During the war, and for years afterwards, an important, and much appreciated, war charity of the Commonwealth countries was the sending of food parcels to friends and relatives in the United Kingdom, and this practice continued well into the 1950s.

Obviously, qualified people in any field were in short supply. The production of university graduates in all countries was restricted in the war years, in some countries there had been a complete cessation.

Those with qualifications were in demand (in addition to career employment) for staffing universities and other training institutions in the home countries, and many of the colonial Territories were establishing universities, or, as in Malaya, extending existing facilities, to enable them to be self-sufficient for the supply of 'trained' personnel. At the time of independence in 1957, the Division I section of the Government Service, which comprised senior appointments in the administration and professional branches, was about 300 short of the establishment of about 3,000, of which total about a third had been filled by local appointees. Whatever deficiencies could be noted in the Government Services, it is obvious that the progress achieved was quite remarkable under all the circumstances.

A view expressed in several quarters in the post-war years was that the Japanese occupation of the area known pre-war as French Indo-China, the Dutch East Indies, and Malaya had hastened the achievement of independence by those countries. As far as Malaya is concerned, I doubt this conclusion, and suggest that events would have proceeded more smoothly, and the foundations for sound administration after independence would have been better established, if normal peace time conditions had continued. As far as education is concerned, seven peaceful years from 1942 to 1949 would have seen much progress as the fabric of a good education system, adapted to the needs of the country and its people, was well established, and each year would have seen further advances, as the value of the facilities in existence were more generally understood. As it was, the seven years were spent in widespread destruction, and in rapid rehabilitation, in equal periods, the latter period being under enormous pressure of the vastly increased demand for schooling which appeared post-war. This had the appearance of the sudden explosion of pent-up demand forcibly denied during the war years; seven years of steady progress would surely have reached the same position much more efficiently and happily.

For those who were directly involved in the process, the most remarkable feature of the course of events was the rapidity with which one stage followed another; writing now 45 years after Malayan independence, my main impression is the sudden impact of the changes, and wonder at how much was done in such a short span of years, and generally done well enough for rational and orderly developments to follow. This was despite some quite dramatic crises, which arose from the complex racial make-up of the country, and the volatile international situation which is inevitable from the country's position. The region is comprised of countries which all, except Thailand, have had recent and differing experiences of the change from colonial times to independence. But at the time of writing, the constitutional and economic condition of the country (Malaysia) still bears a recognisable likeness to that launched at independence in 1957, a not very common feature of many former colonial Territories at present.

As our last three years' service were spent during the first three years of Malayan independence, something needs to be recorded concerning the conditions for European officers during the period. Complex problems and situations can best be understood if they are reduced to simple and basic terms, where this is possible. In our situation on the eve of Malayan independence the conditions were only too simple. At the date of independence, all European officers would be given compulsory retirement, under agreed conditions of compensation, and the Public Service would be staffed entirely, at all levels, by local Malayan people. But, in practical terms, an immediate departure of all European officers was seen to be impossible, and arrangements were made to phase out the departure of the Europeans to ensure that the changeover was made as smoothly as possible. The period for which the government wished to retain the European officers was stated for each department. The European officers could apply to retire at any date after 1 July 1957. The actual date for independence was set for 31 August 1957.

The above was the view of the government. But the situation of each serving European officer was of course different; for many the circumstances differed very widely. In effect each officer was given a stated period of years to arrange for future employment, essential for most of us, and to make suitable provision for our families, many of whom were of school age. Even senior officers, near the normal retiring age, had to bring forward their plans in some degree. For those who required to start another career in employment, it is obvious that the sooner a start was made the more likely a suitable position might be obtained. Another important difference arose from the occupation of the officers; clearly those in professions, such as medicine, engineering, teaching, or the law could have qualifications valid for appointment in most western countries; civil servants with no professional qualifications faced more difficulty.

As has been indicated in this account, most European officers, and most of their wives, developed a real attachment to the country, so that our departure came as something of an emotional wrench. Typical comments heard by me at the time were:

'I should like to stay for a while. I am interested to see what happens in the country.'

'I shall stay as long as conditions are bearable.'
'I shall stay until I am thrown out.'

As far as Yvonne and I were concerned, life proceeded after independence much as it had done before; certainly our personal and official relationships with the people we worked with were unchanged. The real problem, of course, was in the political activities of the newly elected Federation Parliament and the State Councils; the Federation Parliament had been in existence just over two years, the State Councils much less, and that in Selangor, for instance, only a few months. As mentioned earlier, my departure from Pahang followed political action by the newly elected council. A common desire on the part of the new politicians was to criticise, sometimes without making any attempt to understand the situation complained of. The reader may infer that a possible motive in the Pahang incident was to make a counter-diversion in respect of my strong, not to say ruthless, action regarding the Pekan English school. This action of course had been done with the support of the sultan and the Chief Minister, who were understandably furious at the outcome. In this case my successor was another European who made a point of continuing my policies, and the Alliance caucus were given a lesson, which I had reason to believe was communicated to other States. Six months before independence in August 1957, the federal government did not want a crisis in any State Council.

Our departure from Selangor was possibly hastened by another curious incident. Without prior notice or consultation, Yvonne received a notice from the Federal Education Department transferring her as lecturer to a new training institute, which was being established to train local teachers in specialist subjects, home science, manual arts, physical education, and other subjects not taught by the ordinary teacher with general training. There were two things of note about this occurrence. Yvonne was not, like myself, employed as a federal official who could be transferred anywhere in the Federation, but a temporary officer employed by the State government. The other aspect was that Yvonne had not been consulted as to whether she wanted to undertake this work. The appointment was in any case quite impossible, under any practical considerations. We had only a maximum of two years' service ahead of us under the Agreement, and some months of this would be spent on home leave, for which we were then due. Yvonne could therefore at most spend 18 months in the new position in a new institution, in which she would have had to undertake the writing of syllabuses and the multifarious duties of the administration of a new teaching department.

She would leave the position at the time when it would have just commenced functioning, to be followed by a successor who would almost certainly be a newly qualified graduate – if indeed at the time a replacement was available.

This incident illustrates a common situation following the upheaval consequent upon major political changes. Just before independence the Federal Education Department asked if I would agree to my senior inspector of Malay schools being transferred to a similar post in the federal headquarters. Of course I agreed, one reason being that I had an excellent teacher who had been with me at Klang High School – competent and held in high regard in his community. Thus the work of the Malay schools in Selangor proceeded efficiently. Perhaps the need for careful and full consultation is the most important thing for persons new in administration to understand; and understanding comes slowly.

The official aim of the Malayan Government in continuing to employ some expatriate officers stated that 'an important part of their task must be to train their Malayan successors'. But much of the desire for independence sprang from a widespread attitude, not only among the politicians, to try to do things differently, and *not* to follow the established practices of the British. This opinion was not held by most of the local officers with whom we worked, who were only too grateful to receive all the advice and assistance we could give, literally to our last day of duty.

Some comments have been made about the onset of independence as it appeared to us at the time we left the country, but at this point an assessment can be given of the contemporary situation in our experience. On the one hand there was a keen desire that education and training should develop as rapidly as possible, so that the country should be well supplied with qualified people to run the public service and also to foster local industry when the expatriate personnel had left the country. But there is no doubt, in my opinion, that there was a tide of opinion which was demanding independence at the earliest possible moment, which of course ran counter to the need to ensure that the organs of government were working efficiently.

Most importantly, the demand for independence was widespread in every colonial Territory to the exclusion of all other considerations – it was like a huge tide, or mighty ocean current, which flows on inexorably, quite obliterating everything in its path. This movement has been widespread throughout the twentieth century and has been viewed as overriding any other aspect of policy – independence first and foremost was the aim of every national movement.

Indeed, there is little doubt that even if the twentieth century had been peaceful, the movement towards independence would have proceeded, in my view, much as it has done. Britain is in fact a very small economic base for the vast organisation which constituted the Empire, and increasingly would have become a partner among the group of self-determining states. In retrospect, the verdict of history may well be that the move towards independence could have been more orderly, but in the prevailing conditions at the date of independence might also have been accompanied by more strife and turmoil than in fact occurred. All in all, both the newly independent countries and the departing British administrations were very fortunate in the manner in which the changes were achieved.

Other comments may be made regarding life under the British Empire. British officials filled the senior posts in each Territory, in the earlier years entirely making up the senior section of the administrations, and latterly, in most Territories including Malaya, still responsible for most of the important directions and planning. But our lives were artificial compared with our compatriots in the 'home' countries in one important respect – the need to send children home for schooling from about their eighth year. It is fair to say that in our time there was some disagreement among the officers and their wives and families about this necessity, and some children were kept in Malaya while their parents were on duty, returning home to Britain when each leave period was due. There were schools in Kuala Lumpur that catered for European children, but such schools were not available elsewhere in Malaya. As noted above, our son Mark was able to attend kindergartens before he left the country, while his two sisters were not.

The separations resulting were dealt with in various ways. A common practice was for the mother to stay in the home country after the children reached school age, the officer continuing with his career, and seeing his family during leave periods; sometimes the wives came out to Malaya to be with their husbands for a few months each tour. Obviously there was considerable stress placed on family relationships; we managed to have the girls to stay in the long summer vacation, which at least served to maintain family contact. But Yvonne told me after our retirement that she felt that she did not sleep as well as normally while the girls were away at school. In my opinion this imposition on family life was in itself a serious problem in the conduct and maintenance of British rule in the Territories. That the British Government was as successful as it was is an abiding evidence of the ability and devotion of most of the officials employed.

A brief note is indicated regarding the mention of names of colleagues with whom we were associated. The lack of names has been criticised as a deficiency in some Colonial Service accounts, but the problem arises from the desire to avoid any suggestion of invidious references. I have included in this account names of colleagues with whom I was closely associated over a period. Absolutely no criticism is implied of other contemporaries, many of whom I did not chance to meet at any time.

But our final and lasting impression was of a country and people who were basically happy, looked forward to their future with optimism, and who believed that theirs was one of the more favoured places on the globe. I have mentioned the generally pleasant and relaxed atmosphere in which both official duties and social occasions were performed. But it will no doubt be strange for students of the colonial era in Malaya or of any other colonial Territory to read of the genuine mutual regard which existed so often between people of different classes and races. There are many accounts of the actions of the various races to assist their British official acquaintances even during the dangers and difficulties of the war and the years of the Emergency which followed. Yvonne and I had frequent occasions of kindly and friendly actions; on one Muslim festival, that at the end of the Fasting Month, our Malay driver insisted that we visit his family to join in his celebration, which was held outside his small quarters.

Compared with the time span of some previous civilisations, the British Empire as an organised political entity lasted just three centuries, from the appointment in the 1660s of a Privy Council Committee to oversee colonial enterprises, to the closure of the Colonial Office in 1966. From the early settlements at the beginning of the seventeenth century, accompanied by the establishment of East India Company and other trading companies which developed trade with Russia, the Middle East and various parts of Africa, the British Empire thus had an important influence extending to most parts of the world for four centuries. So the worldwide impact made by the British Empire consisted in a vast range of activity, military, political, economic and social, carried out in a relatively brief compass of years. We may believe that succeeding generations will find much of interest and of abiding value in the records now being compiled.

This influence will have an abiding legacy in the life and development of the countries which once formed its components, as well as for many other countries situated adjacent to areas contained in the Empire. It is the hope of former members of the Colonial Service that their work will be a lasting useful contribution to the countries where they served.

Postscript

Life after leaving Malaya in 1960

My wife and I settled in Perth, Western Australia, where our three children were boarders at local schools. We were fortunate in securing suitable employment until we reached retiring age: Yvonne taught home economics at the school our girls attended, while I, after qualifying, served as a librarian at the university, and finally as librarian of a secondary teachers' college. Our youngest daughter was born shortly after we took up residence in Perth.

After almost 20 years in Perth, we retired to Sydney in 1979, as the more humid and equable climate was recommended on medical advice as a change from the hot and dry climate, and sometimes extreme, variations experienced in Perth. Yvonne died in 1991, after an illness lasting two years.

It is now 2001, and the narrative up to this point is being prepared for publication, unaltered since 1992, except for corrections or minor additions to improve clarity. It is now 40 years since I retired from the Service in Malaya, and an effort has been made throughout to provide enough detailed information to assist a reader who may be unfamiliar with the country, now Malaysia, let alone lacking any knowledge of the years described, from 1946 to 1960.

Many events have occurred in the eight years since 1992 which have directly affected colonies and former colonies, now members of the Commonwealth. First, the last important Territory remaining under British rule, Hong Kong, returned to Chinese sovereignty on 30 June 1997. The remaining overseas possessions which still acknowledge British rule are generally small islands, mostly scattered about the South and North Atlantic and Caribbean, with one former garrison town, Gibraltar, at the entrance to the Mediterranean, and Pitcairn Islands in the Pacific.

Appropriately, the first European country to open relations with Asia, Portugal, was the last to return its remaining colony, Macao, to China in December 1999.

The end of the Empire, and hence of the Colonial and Overseas Civil Services, the Colonial Office (which had actually closed earlier in 1966), of the Corona Club, the social club which held an annual dinner in May during the century for members of the Colonial Service and Colonial Office, was marked by a Special Commemoration in May 1999. This began with a Westminster Abbey service on 25 May 1999, attended by the Queen, at which former members of the services and of the government departments which administered the Empire were present. The service was followed by receptions, held in St James's Palace and Marlborough House, attendance at a Royal Garden Party, and a sundowner at the House of Lords. As not all applicants could be admitted to the service or the following receptions, an effort was made to have every applicant admitted to the later receptions.

Parting comments

Most readers will be aware that since the end of the Second World War there have been widespread changes influencing both the content and presentation of historical works, which now contain wide differences in content. There is also a corresponding range in the views held by authors on historical controversy, and on the nature of history in general.

A few examples and illustrations of this trend in my experience are now offered.

As mentioned above, for several years before independence, and from memory continued afterwards, the Information Department published regularly, at least monthly, a 'digest' in English, of articles or comment in the vernacular press concerning government policy, complaints from readers and criticism of any kind concerning the functions of government. These comments were invaluable, at least because they gave some reflection of attitudes in the ordinary non-English speaking population. In Malaya, this production was no little achievement; all the vernacular press were monitored, and this meant extracts from Malay (in Arabic script), Chinese, and several Indian languages, which each had their own script. From memory, there were at least three important Indian languages – Tamil from the Madras Province, Bengali and Punjabi from people originating in those northern provinces. Again from memory, I remember no item of real importance. I assume that the complaints were really grievances and generally these would have been conveyed direct to the offices concerned. Of course, diatribes on 'colonialism' were standard, and these contained a generally monotonous sequence of similar views.

There was in my reading, however, one exception of quite remarkable interest. This was an article by a Malay, pointing out that the

British were only one of the European powers, that the Malays would have obtained equal advantage from any other, and most interestingly extolling the French who were stated to be actually superior in most aspects.

Thus, before my departure from Malaya, there was ample evidence of the widespread attitude of denigration or belittlement of the British and their policies and achievements in the countries which were colonies in the Empire.

The strength of the surge to independence was well illustrated, as described previously, by the independent action of the Pahang State Alliance – this was six months before the date of independence on 31 August 1957, until which date the British High Commissioner, Sir Donald McGillivray, was still in effective control of the government. It is worth adding that, before his departure as High Commissioner in May 1954, Sir Gerald Templer issued a strong condemnation of any action or statement which in any way was subversive of the actions in Malaya of the 'Protecting Power'. The Malay States and later the Federation came under British rule by treaties with the States; in no sense was British rule due to either conquest or forceful occupation.

It will therefore be understood that I gained little respect for most of these writers or of their productions, which usually presented a one-sided point of view – usually inspired by 'independence politics' or by the accompanying pervasive attitude of 'anti-colonialism'. It is unnecessary to add that much writing of a similar inspiration has been general in Britain and in all English-speaking countries, not least in Australia. And especially it must be emphasised that a similar general attitude has been applied to works on ancient history, classical literature and the Bible.

However, there is much in modern scholarship which fully utilises the solid advances made possible by technical achievements, such as the scientific accurate dating of many archaeological artefacts and the decipherment of ancient scripts.

So, to conclude: the tide is beginning to turn. Scholars are willing once again to look at both sides of the debate (that is, the history of the colonial period and of the Colonial Service).[20]

As to personal relations, much description in this narrative has been given of the generally friendly and cooperative attitude of the people, of all races and ages. It is widely recognised, now that the British Empire has passed into history, that the experience of members of the Colonial Service is unique in that the Service was in itself a career, spent sometimes in one or more Territories, but always under similar conditions. I never felt in any way an 'outsider', employed to undertake specific tasks on a short project, but in every way a member of the Government Service, who worked with and alongside many government staff. These included people of various local races as well as Europeans, and of all ranks, from senior administrative officials to the lower socio-economic levels whose work was invaluable – labourers, drivers or messengers.

On the second and related topic I quickly realised that the excellent attitude I experienced was not a recent occurrence, but built up from the years of British rule by British officials. It seemed to this observer as a British official, that people expected to receive fair treatment, reasonable consideration of the matter raised and some concern for the welfare and well-being of the people affected by government decisions. The really remarkable thing to me was that the government organisation and all the individuals in Government Service, of whatever status, had received a battering in the three and a half years of the Japanese occupation, along with severe deprivation of the necessities of life – especially food.

But in my experience, the Service was always excellent: for instance the devoted expertise of several school clerks, Malays and Indians, and the Sikh chief clerk in the Pahang Education Office, who coped with a massive incoming and outgoing daily mail, and for whom nothing was too much trouble. That the Government Service possessed such people was the foundation of the efficient working of the system; and also most importantly, all the work of government and everyone else in the country was until three years after independence subject to the additional burdens caused by the Communist Insurrection or Emergency.

I look back on my time in Malaya with unchanged attitudes towards my experience of the country, of its people, and of my work with them. In brief, I should not wish to have spent those years anywhere else. But the important thing in my view is the gaining of knowledge and experience, all at first hand, which remains with one as a permanent asset. It is a help towards understanding contemporary events as they unfold, especially regarding the countries of South East Asia.

The rapid development of these countries, from South Korea and Taiwan in the north down to Indonesia in the south, has been a source of interest, not to say amazement for the trading nations of Europe and North America, and not least for their closest neighbours, Australia and New Zealand. The sudden economic decline in the last few years, followed by a slow partial recovery came as an equal surprise, even something of a shock, to traders in those overseas countries. Obviously, it was not widely appreciated in western countries how brief the experience of the Asian countries as modern international traders has been, in contrast to the long and gradual development of those overseas countries over previous centuries.

It is my hope that mutual understanding between all these countries will continually improve in the years ahead, with abiding and substantial benefit to each country and especially to their populations.

Appendix 1
Migration and travel:
historical note

It is not often in history that migration and settlement, in countries other than that of a person's birth, is readily possible. In Malaya, the mixture of very different races and cultures proceeded for many years without restriction, the resulting community being peaceful and orderly.

National and racial identity, as a political factor in the international scene, is the prevalent and overriding consideration at the present time. The reader may, for instance, compare Malaya prior to 1942 with the countries described in the New Testament. In the first century AD, the Roman Empire was at its 'Golden Age', when travel along the great public roads from one end of the Empire to another was relatively safe, by persons of *any* race, and the passage of ships from port to port similarly free from any let or hindrance.

Prior to 1914, passports were not required for travel from Britain to other countries, oddly enough, with the exception of Russia. Industries were established in different colonial Territories with the aid of imported labour, usually Indian. Thus, when the rubber industry was developed in Malaya after 1900, the government arranged to bring Indian labourers from Madras to provide labour for the new industry, Malays not being interested in daily labour for wages. About the same time, Indians were brought to Fiji to work the new sugar estates. The Chinese had migrated to Malaya for centuries, as traders and tin miners, and when British rule was established after 1880 in the Malay States, Chinese immigration increased greatly.

When war broke out with Japan in 1941, the Chinese and Indian populations together equalled that of the Malays. The immigrants lived peaceably, and in daily life they tended to confine their association to their own people, for example separate Chinese and Tamil schools being established.

After some years' work in Malaya, the Chinese and Indians tended to return to their home countries, taking with them the money which they had accumulated.

This system of temporary immigration of course ceased with the Japanese occupation, and after the war India became independent in 1947 and the Communists seized control of China in 1949. The result was a change to permanent residence for a large proportion of the Chinese and Indian populations in Malaya.

At the date of Independence in 1957, all residents who had been for some years continuously in the country were given the option of taking out Malayan citizenship, which meant that as citizens they had voting rights in elections and access to civil rights on equal terms with those born in the country. The fact that this mass admission to citizenship was carried out without difficulty was one of the major achievements which took place at Independence, to which the resulting cohesion of the different races contributed greatly in furthering communal stability.

Appendix 2
Colonisation and assisted immigrants

Mention has been made that colonies, in the original classical sense of communities organised in lands remote from the original countries, have been developed extensively, as a matter of deliberate policy, by only the Greeks, during the eighth to sixth centuries BC and in modern times by the British from about 1600 AD to the twentieth century up to the Second World War.

There are qualifications to this general statement. The Romans, who gave us the word 'colonia', established numerous settlements in different parts of the Empire from discharged soldiers with their families as 'strong points' whose existence helped to maintain peace and stability where they were established. But in no sense were these military settlements important as places of settlement. The trading post, Quebec, established by the French in North America, is today a populous and thriving community. The Dutch, from about 1600, established Cape Town as a half-way provisioning port for their ships sailing to and from their wealthy colony of mercantile importance, the East Indies. The Portuguese took possession of Goa in India, Malacca in the Malay Peninsula and Macao in China, from which they controlled the trade between Asia and Europe during the sixteenth century. The Spanish conquered and exploited the American continent from Mexico to Patagonia, except for Brazil which was a Portuguese sphere of trade.

But establishing a national colony as a viable entity in a foreign territory calls for considerable skills of planning, organisation and knowledge of the site of settlement. The Greek colonies, over a thousand of them, were usually quite tiny, of a few hundred people, who required selection to produce a viable self-supporting entity. But the Mediterranean has a very similar climate throughout, so the colonists had the main task in each site of obtaining the acquiescence and cooperation of the existing inhabitants. Usually this was not too difficult, as the Greeks, the most civilised people of the time, could provide advantages in trade and useful products, such as pottery.

The British moved to sites remote from their home country. They had to find out the nature of the climate and production capacity of the land, and provide the capital and skilled persons to set up the buildings, industries and adjacent ports where supplies could be landed, and goods exported. Above all, an adequate labour force to carry out the daily tasks was required to maintain a viable economic entity.

The establishment of the workforce was the greatest and continuing problem in every colony. The working classes at home had no resources to pay for their voyage to the colony and had to be persons able to undertake the tasks required. In the colony, there had to be provision of work to employ and support the workforce economically. The majority of settlers in the first years of Virginia and Massachusetts died. Quite early in Virginia, slaves and convicts were introduced to work the plantations. The free immigrants were generally brought in as indentured servants, who were guaranteed to work for their employers at least a number of years.

The Australasian colonies, apart from the convict settlements of Sydney and Tasmania, received a fortuitous boost in the gold rushes which brought large numbers of immigrants to the goldfields of Victoria, and some arrivals to the fields in New South Wales, Queensland and New Zealand. South Australia and Western Australia were established by corporate bodies which selected colonists and organised the communities in the new colonies. Several settlements in New Zealand were also founded by a corporation, the 'New Zealand Company', which being later than the foundations in Australia, benefited by the experiences of the earlier settlements. The latest settlement, Christchurch (1850) was planned in every detail – temporary sheds were built at the port of arrival to accommodate the settlers while they were assigned the sites of their houses and businesses. The complement of colonists included persons skilled in each trade, teachers and professional people, and as it was promoted by the Church of England, a bishop and clergy. Such was the progress achieved by the hard, often tragic, experiences from the first settlement in Virginia in 1607 and later settlements in America and elsewhere.

As the colonies were established, and industries were developed, the Australasian colonies organised schemes for 'assisted immigrants' from Britain. Prospective applicants were interviewed by Colonial Government agents, the passages of selected immigrants paid by the receiving colony and provision made for employment and accommodation with an employer on arrival. Of course, these schemes operated only during years of good economic conditions. In New Zealand, the scheme operated from about 1870 to the early 1880s, when my maternal grandparents migrated. The scheme ceased during the severe depression from about 1885 to 1895, and was revived after 1900 when my father arrived accompanied by two sisters and two brothers.

The European population of each colony, including the American colonies on the eve of independence, was made up of more than 50 per cent of people descended from assisted immigrants. The importance of these assisted immigrants in the establishment of these countries is beyond estimation.

Appendix 3
New Zealand secondary schools

It will be noted that I received my secondary education at a small country high school, from which I qualified to enter university and also gained a university scholarship. At this time, it was compulsory for all Arts degree students to include a foreign language, usually French, as a degree subject. It was also necessary for law and medical students to pass the matriculation examination in Latin. Thus all secondary schools were required to have a qualified teacher in French and Latin, to enable the students to qualify in these subjects.

These small high schools had enrolments of about 300, about half boys and half girls, compared with those in the large provincial centres and cities which would total at least twice as many students, in separate schools for boys and girls. Of course, these larger schools were able to offer considerable advantages – larger and more varied staffs, wider sports facilities, and a number of extra-mural activities such as drama, music with a school orchestra, debating, a variety of arts subjects, and so on. But in the main and essential work of classroom teaching, quite often the advantage lay with the smaller schools. Schools in the larger towns and cities tended to be those where teachers spent the rest of their careers, and hence tended to be conservative and less attuned to new developments – in education or in the community.

Thus staffs in the small schools were often composed of teachers fresh from university, keen to progress in their skills, without having the restraints of tradition. I was in fact taught English by a senior mistress with honours in the subject, and history by a first-class honours woman graduate. At the present time, teachers with these qualifications would generally aim to join a university staff.

The geography of New Zealand also has a major influence. A glance at the map will indicate that the country consists of two small islands but each includes many ranges of mountains and high hills, which make surface communication difficult and expensive to maintain. Hence the districts, large or small, strive to be as self-contained as possible for economic life, education, entertainment and sporting activities. Even today, those living in or near towns of, say, five thousand or so, rarely have to go to the larger centres except for special needs not locally available.

Appendix 4

Education in Malaya, 1941: records and documents

A basic problem in writing on education in Malaya after the Second World War is that pre-war records were entirely destroyed during the Japanese occupation. In general terms, staffs who had been employed in the years up to 1941 of course had a good recollection of pre-war conditions in so far as their experience went, but usually this experience was confined to one State or Settlement.

I will give one example of the completeness of destruction by the Japanese. Any education system must be carried out under provisions of detailed law and regulations, which in Malaya was known as the 'Education Code'. On the resumption of British government in September 1945, no copy of this document could be found. A senior education official, F.C. Barraclough (referred to in this narrative), produced the 'Code' verbatim completely from memory, so that it could be reprinted and issued to all schools and education offices. By such means, it was possible to ensure that the operation of the Education Department post-war carried on the procedures followed pre-war.

Of course, pre-war official annual reports and other records, normally produced each year by most education systems, were also completely missing. So the Malayan Education Department pursued an initiative of copying articles on Malayan education which had been published in *Overseas Education* (the education journal published by the Colonial Office), in the years preceding the war, and publishing them in a separate pamphlet, for issue to schools and education offices.[21]

It so happened that the most senior pre-war education official, H.R. Cheeseman, CMG, the pre-war Deputy Director of Education, who had survived internment in Changi gaol and was then over retiring age, was appointed Director of Education for the first two years or so after the resumption of civil government. He had served in Malaya for a total of 40 years, a most exceptional total of service for any official in the Colonial Service. Mr. Cheeseman's range of experience of course enabled him to pronounce readily on any matter or circumstance that came up for decision. He had arrived in Penang in 1907 as a pupil teacher in an aided school, which was later taken over by the government, and service in responsible positions followed.

Included in this pamphlet was an address by the acting Director of Education, A.W. Frisby, on 22nd March 1946, giving details of progress in the rehabilitation of the schools in the six months since the Japanese surrender in September 1945. He gave these figures:

Total enrolment	1941	1946
English-medium schools	61,000	80,000
Malay vernacular schools	128,000	125,000
Chinese schools	121,000	128,000
Indian schools	26,000	16,000[22]
All types of schools, Singapore and Malaya	336,000	350,000[23]

As civil government resumed on 1 April 1946, this was the effective enrolment of the schools when civil government took over.

Appendix 5
Education of girls in Malaya

The change in attitude to education by all races in Malaya, and by all classes, was the most striking change evident in the community when the British returned following the Japanese surrender in September 1945. The change was so marked as to herald a revolution; whereas pre-war the provision of education was almost entirely at the inspiration as well as the direction of Europeans.

After 1945, the problem was coping with the demand from all sections of the community, which clamoured for educational facilities appropriate to each race and to each locality. True, school was compulsory for Malay boys for four years since the First World War in all States, but for the other races education was voluntary. Generally, attendance declined markedly in the upper primary classes, and this was particularly true of the girls, who enrolled at about half the number of the boys. As a result, girls formed on average only a quarter of the total enrolments, and by 1941 this proportion was being attained by Malay girls.

But the real surprise when the children lined up for the first enrolment was the number of girls present – often about equal in number to that of the boys. The situation was similar for the children of labourers and peasants in the villages to that of the families of shopkeepers and clerks in the towns, where they formed the majority of the new entrants. It is therefore worth noting the previous history of female education in Malaya. In brief, that there had previously been many fewer girls than boys was not due to lack of trying, either by government education officials, or more commonly by members of the teaching orders of various churches. A Church of England school in Singapore did pioneer service of many years before 1900, and a government school, Raffles Girls' School, was established about the same time, and similarly battled on against the prevailing 'prejudice and conservatism' of the community.[24]

The girls' English schools are therefore the creation of the twentieth century, most being established by the Catholic orders, the American Methodist Episcopal Mission, the Church of England

and one Brethren mission school. All were established in their early years by direct approach of the teachers concerned to prospective parents – doctors, lawyers and businessmen. If this was the situation with educated families, what chance was there for girls of labourers, peasants, stall-holders or truck drivers?

By 1941, the situation had therefore developed to the stage where the enrolment of girls in the English schools was about half that of the boys. Malay girls were, however, just beginning to attend English schools and numbered only about 10 per cent of the Malay boys' enrolment in these schools. Only the Eurasians enrolled their girls on a similar footing to the boys; right from the establishment of the first English girls' school, Eurasians formed the mainstay of the staffs in these schools, which ensured that the standards in these schools were the highest in the country.

As indicated above, attendance of girls in the vernacular schools, Malay, Chinese and Indian, was proportionately similar, girls not remaining at school for as long as the boys.

It must be realised that the educational situation stems directly from the social and economic nature of the Asian family. Children, both boys and girls, are a primary economic asset in each family, and as soon as they are old enough, contribute to the economic maintenance of the family. Thus it is useful for the boys to be literate and numerate – in a small Chinese shop or business, a quite young boy will take your order, write out the invoice, and calculate the price, giving the correct change. Girls, however, are more limited to household tasks – cooking and sewing, or going out into the fields to assist with crop supervision, for which literacy or numeracy skills are not so essential.

After the war, it was suddenly realised that girls who had at least basic literacy and numeracy skills were employable in shops and in factories, which gave them an economic value in addition to, and usually greater than, what they possessed as members of the family. One illustration of this trend is evident in the supply of good domestic servants, which in our time in the country presented no difficulty. Soon after independence, domestic servants became unobtainable, the women having found that they were better paid as factory hands, for a much shorter working day.

Appendix 6

Cambridge School Certificate examination results, 1946

As indicated earlier in this account, my New Zealand origins were naturally a source of inspiration in my career in Malaya, especially the question of how far I was able to measure up to the standard of my UK colleagues.

The results for my first group of students for the Cambridge School Certificate in 1946 reached us in the March following the December examination. There were few failures – no more than one or two in any subject, and in history only one, by the only boy to fail the whole examination. Of course, the number of 'A' passes was a main interest by the teacher in each subject. In history, there were no 'A' passes, as occurred in other subjects, including English. But in fact, by comparison with other schools, the history results were outstanding. Naturally, this result was a source of satisfaction to me, and it certainly established my reputation in the Service which I was fortunate to retain until my retirement.

The Colonial Service had recruited qualified persons from the then Dominions since the 1920s, and my university calendar in the early 1930s included appointments in the Colonial Service as possible choices of careers for graduates. Of course, an upbringing and education overseas gave those concerned a more familiar and first-hand knowledge of conditions and life generally in those parts of the Empire, British by origin and still similar in tradition, but from an entirely different standpoint from that of those from the British Isles. As will have been noticed by the reader, in the Malayan Education Service my experience so far from being less relevant than that of British colleagues actually in some respects had advantages.

Appendix 7

Domestic science in Malay schools

By 1941, the girls had reached about 25 per cent of the total Malay school enrolments. In general, Perak was the most 'advanced' state, and domestic science was introduced into the Malay schools in 1929, with the appointment of a European domestic science mistress.[25]

Malay women pupil teachers received courses in teaching domestic science, and as they qualified, domestic science centres were established in the Malay girls' schools. Progress was recorded as follows: in 1929, four centres; in 1930, seven centres; in 1934, thirty-three centres; and in 1939, fifty-four centres out of sixty-two girls' schools, and in four centres in mixed schools. There was also some progress in teaching domestic science in Malay girls' schools in Selangor.

Thus, though the equipment, lesson material and organisation disappeared during the Japanese occupation, there remained a recollection of the 'good days' pre-war and a widespread desire to re-establish pre-war standards as soon as possible.

Appendix 8
Pahang State

On a re-reading of this account, some explanation as a background to the events seems desirable. As indicated frequently in this work, all the States in Malaya had their own individual qualities and, needless to say, special problems. These arose from the history of the people in the State and their social, political and economic history. As stated above, Pahang had perhaps more difficulties than any other State, owing to its large area and mountainous topography with the attendant lack of reliable communications.

Only the larger towns and the villages adjacent to each route were connected by all-weather roads; the Malay population was largely confined to the river banks, and the rivers were their sole means of communication with the larger centres. The mining towns and rubber estates were of course served by reliable roads, and their populations were mainly Chinese or Indians. The recently constructed railway ran from the south up the middle of the State to the east coast, and for most of the way was not served by any road.

Many Malay villages had no access except by footpath through miles of jungle; I inspected one Malay school after parking the car on the main road, then walking about four miles to the village. For the record, it was as efficient a school as could be imagined; the four teachers and hundred odd pupils were happy – and rightly proud of their school. Of course, the people were prosperous in a very fertile area.

To sum up, the population of the State was scattered widely in small cultivable plots, and the problems of communication, on which any government must rely, were in large part insuperable. Even under favourable conditions, economic progress obviously had to be slow.

Therefore, it comes as no surprise that the political history of Pahang is perhaps the most confused of the Malay States. Most armed insurrections in the States arose from dynastic quarrels. From 1857 to 1863, a civil war arose in Pahang when two brothers fought for the throne.[26]

Pahang was the last of the Federated Malay States to sign a treaty accepting British advice and assistance; in fact British assistance was required as late as 1880 to enable an insurrection to be quelled. Obviously, joining the Federated Malay States in 1890 gave the State Government a useful 'sheet anchor' for stability.

Thus, the action of the Alliance in 'going their own way' without consultation with the government was unexpected, but certainly no new political aberration in Pahang.

Appendix 9
Bibliographical note

As will have been evident throughout this account, I was, during the entire period of my service in Malaya, an extensive reader of the available literature on the history of Malaya, as well as of works dealing with the politics, Islamic religion and social customs related to the Malay population. To complete the Stage III Government Malay Examination required wide and intensive study of published material in both English and Malay. The library of the Sultan Idris Tanjong Malim (Malay Men's) Training College was especially valuable, and I was fortunate in having access to this collection during my time at the college.

One important, indeed unique, circumstance must be borne in mind in considering any aspect of government and education after the British return to Malaya in 1945: the Japanese throughout their occupation were ruthless in their policy of attempting to expunge every trace of the English language and all published material in English existing anywhere in the country at the onset of war and invasion. All English textbooks in the schools were destroyed, and all records in the offices of the Education Departments were systematically put to oblivion. To give two examples, the 'Education Code', which contained the regulations for the conduct of the schools, was, as stated earlier, rewritten from memory by a senior education officer, F.C. Barraclough, as not a single copy could be found post-war. The annual reports of the department, which contained detailed information and statistics up to the war, had also disappeared, and the information could only be obtained by reprinting the required material from copies in the Colonial Office in London.

In fact, however, much of the pre-war official and education stock of publications was secreted for the duration of the occupation by members of the Government Services, needless to say at great risk to their lives if there was any discovery by the Japanese secret police. I never heard of any instance of discovery; indeed, when I arrived at King Edward VII School Taiping in June 1946, a very large proportion of the school library books were in the library, having been retrieved by the pre-war staff.

So, to sum up, the body of published material now existing is derived from reprinting of works which survived the war, followed by the production of publications from the British return to the present.

Obviously, for the purposes of this account, only material available during my period of service is relevant.

The Journal of the Malaysian Branch of the Royal Asiatic Society (JMBRAS) is by far the most comprehensive source for material on all aspects of the Malay Peninsula and the adjacent territories. The journal was published in Singapore from 1878 to 1922 as the *Journal of the Straits Branch of the Royal Asiatic Society* (JSBRAS).

In 1878 only the Colony of the Straits Settlements (Singapore, Penang and Malacca) was under British rule, except Perak from 1874. Gradually, the nine Malay States came under British rule as 'Protected States', from Perak in 1874 to Johore in 1913, in each case by a formal treaty with the British Government. During this time, the Society steadily increased its membership in the Malay States, until in 1923, the title changed to the *Journal of the Malayan Branch of the Royal Asiatic Society* 'Malayan' was changed to 'Malaysian' when the Federation changed its name after the addition of the former British Colonies of North Borneo and Sarawak in 1963.

The importance of the journal as a source of information on the history and peoples of the region therefore cannot be exaggerated. The foundation of the Society in 1878 was only four years after Perak became the first Protected Malay State in 1874. From the outset many British officials, mainly in the administrative and education branches contributed works of the highest standard of scholarship, increasingly supplemented over the years by writers of all races in the region. The Society and its journal continue to flourish; increasingly contributors include members of universities overseas who have interests in aspects of the history and people of the region.

In 1963, the journal published an 'Index Malaysiana' including all publications of the journal since 1878. This index is updated by supplements, No. 1 covering 1964–1973 and No. 2, 1974–1983. In addition to the journal, the Society has throughout its history published monographs on Malaysian topics, many of which are kept in print.

The address of the MBRAS office is:

130M (Mezzanine Floor)
Jalan Tamby Abdullah
Off Jalan Tun Sambanthan
(Brickfields) 50470
Kuala Lumpur
West Malaysia

The definitive history of the Colonial Service is *On Crown Service: a History of H.M. Colonial and Overseas Civil Services, 1837–1997*, by Anthony Kirk-Green, London, I.B. Tauris, 1999. The author served in Nigeria for many years in the Colonial Service. He is Emeritus Fellow of St Anthony's College, Oxford.

A comprehensive collection of contributions by former members of the Colonial Service, and by others who lived in the colonies under the British Empire, is kept in Rhodes House Library, Oxford, under the Oxford Development Records Project, to which this account will be forwarded. The collection now numbers many books, memoirs and papers by former Colonial Service officers. Two by contemporary colleagues in my possession are *Out East in the Malay Peninsula*, by G.E.D. Lewis, Petaling Jaya, Malaysia, Penerbit Fajar Bakti Sdn Bhd, 1991.

Dr Lewis served in the Malayan Education Department from June 1938 to September 1962, including experience in Thailand on the infamous Siam railway. From 1956 until his retirement, he was headmaster of Victoria Institution, Kuala Lumpur, the oldest and the leading government English school in Malaya. As chief education officer, Selangor, 1957–1960, I of course became well acquainted with him. The other is by Christopher Blake, *A View from Within*, Castle Cary, Somerset, Mendip Publishing, 1990. Christopher Blake arrived with the British Army of Occupation in 1945 and served till he retired from the Administrative Service in 1958. For some years he was district officer in the district where Tanjong Malim is situated, when I was acting as principal of the Malay Men's Teaching College in Tanjong Malim.

Government publications

As stated above, these were reprints from reports held by the Colonial Office, London. I have used the following: *Education in Malaya*, Kuala Lumpur, Government Printer, 1948 and *Education in Malaya 1941*, Government Printer, rep. 1946 from *Overseas Education 1941* copy held in the Colonial Office, London (journal published by the Colonial Office). Also of importance in studying the history of Malaysia is *The Malays, a Cultural History*, by Richard Winstedt, Singapore, Kelly and Walsh, 1947. Sir Richard Winstedt was a senior member of the Administrative Service and British Resident, the senior British official in Johore in his last post. He was a leading scholar on the Malays, their culture, religion and language. After his retirement, he continued his career in Malay scholarship and was President of the Royal Asiatic Society of Great Britain and Ireland. He was a prominent and regular contributor to the *Journal of the MBRAS* and its predecessor *Journal of the SBRAS*. As well as many works on the history of Malaya and on individual States, Dr Winstedt has written extensively on Malay language and literature, and produced Malay dictionaries and students' texts.

A contemporary writer on Malaysia and its history is John M. Gullick, who arrived in Malaya with the British Military Administration after the Japanese surrender in 1945 and transferred to the Malayan Civil Service in 1946, with which he served until his retirement in 1956. The *Journal of the MBRAS*, Vol. 72, part 2, Dec. 1999 was published as a 'Festschrift' and includes a complete list of his publications. Two examples are *A History of Selangor, 1766–1939*, MBRAS Monograph No. 28, 1998 and *A History of Kuala Lumpur, 1857–1939*, MRAS Monograph (forthcoming). The 'Festschrift' fittingly records a distinguished career as civil servant and author. *Templer, Tiger of Malaya*, by John Cloake, London, Harrap, 1985, is a complete biography of Sir Gerald Templer, but a third of the book gives a detailed (and graphic) account of Templer as High Commissioner of Malaya from 1952 to 1954, when a successful policy on the Emergency was of prime, and even capital, importance.

New Zealand and Australia

My early life in New Zealand and references to Australia, which has been my place of residence since 1960, have been noted at various points in this account.

As detailed above, from its foundation in 1874, the MBRAS has fostered a scholarly survey of the history of Malaysia and of adjacent regions, from the earliest times to contemporary events.

In New Zealand, European settlement was largely the result of early missionary activity and of the Corporation New Zealand

Company, which organised directly or indirectly most of the settlements in both islands from 1840. The exception was Auckland,
which was designated the capital by the government. After the first
appointment of Governor Hobson in 1840, who arranged the Treaty
of Waitangi with the Maori chiefs, New Zealand was separated from
New South Wales in 1841.

An early governor, Sir George Grey, was keenly interested and
skilled in understanding the Maori race and language, the results
of which form a substantial literature. A Maori dictionary,
still accepted as definitive, was the work of an Anglican Bishop
Williams. There are therefore several generally accepted works on
New Zealand history, which differ essentially only on interpretation
of generally accepted accounts of events.

New Zealand is in great contrast to Australia in every respect, the
only similarity being its origin from direct British settlement, its
establishment in the late 1830s being about 50 years after the
settlement of Sydney in 1788. Comparing the two countries,
New Zealand is quite tiny, being about equivalent to Victoria with
Tasmania. New Zealand has a cool to mild climate, with ample to
heavy rainfall, which falls fairly evenly throughout the year. The
drier districts on the east coast are able to support a varied agriculture. Perhaps, most importantly, the native Maori population
constitute a large minority – the Maoris number about twice the total
of the Australian Aboriginals. They form therefore a very considerable portion of the smaller population of New Zealand. The Maoris
have very greatly influenced the course of New Zealand history since
the arrival of the Europeans, not least on account of full-scale wars
fought in the 1840s and 1860s over much of the North Island.

A History of New Zealand, by Keith Sinclair, 4th rev. ed.,
Auckland, Penguin Books, 1991 is a good introduction. Sir Keith
Sinclair retired as Professor of History at the University of Auckland
in 1990. The up-to-date text is followed by an exhaustive bibliog-
raphy including writers on pre-European Maori history, early voyages of discovery and subsequent history from the first European
settlements of traders and missionaries.

Australia

The original six colonies had separate origins and development
which largely remain as the distinguishing characters of the six
States. Sydney, New South Wales (1788) and Hobart, Tasmania
(1804) were founded as convict settlements. As population inhabited
those areas, Victoria (1851) and Queensland (1859) separated from

New South Wales. Western Australia (1829) and South Australia (1834) were settled by colonists organised directly from London by corporate bodies. South Australia was settled by a company organised by Edward Gibbon Wakefield, who also founded the New Zealand Company. The distances between the settlements ensured strong individualism – for example the railway gauges differed, so trains could not cross colonial boundaries. Perth is the most isolated city of European origin in the world – it is further from Adelaide, its nearest neighbour, than Sydney is from Auckland.

For many years, conditions of life were such that very little objective historical account of events occurred. The late eighteenth century was still a period when life for the majority was hard, expectancy of life uncertain, and legal procedure and punishments often brutal. But in fact, the settlers in New South Wales, convicts and free settlers, were immensely better off than the inhabitants of industrial cities in England. Arthur Phillip lost very few passengers on the long voyage of the First Fleet. From the beginning, deaths were few in the settlement – the settlers were able to find food from local plants to supplement shortages in the rations. Children born in Sydney grew to increased height and physique compared with their contemporaries in England. The writing of Australian history is therefore subject to constant revision and development, from any of its constituent parts. One example of recent revision and research is *Botany Bay*[27] *Mirages*, by Alan Frost, Carlton, Vic., Melbourne University Press, 1994. Alan Frost is Professor of History at La Trobe University, Melbourne.

Notes

1 See Appendix 9 'Bibliographical note'.

2 See Appendix 1 'Migration and travel: historical note'.

3 In two years the colony was producing enough food to feed the starving arrivals of the Second Fleet, June 1790, and also to feed arrivals of the Third Fleet, August–October 1791; even in the earliest years there were few deaths, and improved health among adults and children. The climate of Sydney impressed the colonists as being pleasant and healthy (Alan Frost, *Botany Bay Mirages*, Carlton, Vic.: Melbourne University Press, 1994.)

4 See Appendix 2 'Assisted immigrants'.

5 See Appendix 3 'New Zealand secondary schools'.

6 A bridge has now connected the island with the peninsula for some years.

7 M.R. Holgate, director from 1948 to 1950.

8 See Appendix 4 'Education in Malaya, 1941: records and documents'.

9 See Appendix 5 'Education of girls in Malaya'.

10 The independence of India, in effect its partition between India and Pakistan, was to take place in August 1947. The 6th Indian Division returned to India in the previous April.

11 See Appendix 6 'Cambridge School Certificate examination results, 1946'.

12 See Appendix 7 'Domestic science in Malay schools'.

13 Another report stated the three men were stationed on two neighbouring estates.

14 Actually, the communist guerrillas held out in camps north of the Thai border until 1989. Then they ceremoniously stacked their weapons to indicate their hostilities had ceased when the news of the destruction of the Berlin Wall appeared.

15 FMS was the usual abbreviation for Federated Malay States.

16 MCS – Malayan Civil Service (the Administrative Service).

17 In Pahang, the Muslim working week, Sunday–Thursday, closing Friday for weekly prayers, was observed only by the Malay schools.

18 An alliance of the United Malay National Organisation (UMNO), Malaysian Chinese Association (MCA) and Malayan Indian Congress (MIC).

[19] See Appendix 8 'The Pahang State Council'.

[20] Anthony Kirk-Greene, *On Crown Service*, London, I.B.Tauris, 1999, p. 110.

[21] *Education in Malaya*, Kuala Lumpur, Government Printer, 1948.

[22] The Indian community suffered more than any other during the Japanese occupation – from privations, diseases and deliberate acts of brutality. The enrolments in the schools are an indication of the total decrease in the Indian population during the war.

[23] The rehabilitation of school buildings and equipment, the provision of textbooks, and the training of teachers of course did not keep up with the enrolment. It took several years for an adequate standard to be reached in these respects.

[24] H.R. Cheeseman, 'Education in Malaya' in *Education in Malaya*, Kuala Lumpur, Government Printer, 1948.

[25] M.C. Taylor, 'Domestic science in Malay girls' schools in Perak', in *Education in Malaya*, Kuala Lumpur, Government Printer, 1948, pp. 105–109.

[26] Richard Winstedt, *The Malays, a cultural history*, Singapore, 1947, p. 156.

[27] Botany Bay was the name given to the bay where Cook visited in 1770, but Arthur Phillip took the First Fleet north to the better site of Port Jackson, where Sydney was established. For many years, however, Botany Bay was the colloquial name for New South Wales. As a postscript, it was a not disgruntled or despondent community whose entire population lined vantage points in Sydney Harbour to farewell Governor Macquarie in 1822.

INDEX